M000191967

This book is more than a personal testimony. It is that, but it is complimented with beautiful poetry and life events that many of us will recognize and can identify with. There is pain and discomfort in this life, but when we get to know His voice. His grace, and strength become sufficient, and His mercies are renewed every morning.

Thank you, Faun.

—Apostol Pappas MD.

Jesus said in John 16:33 KJV:

"These things I have spoken unto you, that in me ye might have peace. In the world ye shall have tribulation: but be of good cheer; I have overcome the world."

Faun Collett has been a gift to my life. She has exemplified a simple yet powerful relationship to Jesus Christ. That has resulted in a wide impact on other people. She has a prophetic ministry as a poet. Only with a gift from God could she write such helpful and meaningful prose. It is fitting that she was called the "Dog Whisperer" and now the "Jesus Whisperer." Her ability to train dogs to do everything but tap dance is amazing, but her real impact is on people. May her book impact you as her life has impacted mine.

—Pastor Terry Roberts

This book is full of *inspired words* from the Lord that Faun has written over the years. Her ability to take what the Lord puts in her heart and articulate it in a way that is full of love, life, compassion, and so much meaning is genuinely inspiring. Faun truly has a rare gift as her writing is a combination of poetry, song and story-telling. I would say that Faun is like a modern-day psalmist, depicted by the beautiful way she writes. This book will take you to places of rejoicing, laughter, encouragement, and most certainly, a closer walk with the Lord.

—Pastor Alex Pappas
Oceans Unite Christian Center

Some people, like Faun Collet, the author of *The Jesus Whisperer,* come into our lives and touch our hearts, and the imprint forever stays with us. The love of the Father flows so easy through the spirit that God put in Faun's heart. She uses His Word to change us and draw us into a relationship with Him, and that is evident in the pages of *The Jesus Whisperer.* No matter what Faun has gone through in life, her love for our heavenly Father flows beautifully from God's Word to your heart, if you would only receive it. Trials, tribulations, and victories are woven throughout her book, and her teaching and encouraging words lets the reader know that they are not alone in this earthly journey. In *The Jesus Whisperer,* she shares from a devoted relationship with the Father. Read and grow in your own walk with Him as she has done. Thank You, Father, for the gift of a friend who knows You intimately and who shares Your written words for direction and healing.

—Pastor Nancy Hart

Faun is one of the most talented people I know. She is full of godly treasures that she has put to pen and paper in her new book, *The Jesus Whisperer,* so that all of us can read and grow spiritually. She loves others with the love of Christ. She would willingly give a stranger her last dollar so that his or her needs could be met. Faun Collet is a self-sacrificing, godly woman, and that is apparent throughout the pages of her book *The Jesus Whisperer.* Enjoy reading this book because it comes from deep within her heart.

—**Pastor Becky,** Faith Christian Family Church

It is with joyful anticipation that I offer this compilation of my life and whisper it onto the pages of this book. My prayer is that these lessons learned will motivate and inspire, and that my skillful Vine Dresser, Jesus Christ, will find another willing vessel to be grafted into the olive tree of eternity.

A man's gift makes room for him, and brings him before great men.

—Proverbs 18:16

The *Jesus Whisperer*

FAUN COLLETT

After the FIRE came a gentle whisper.

—1 Kings 19:12 NIV

WORD & SPIRIT
PUBLISHING

Unless otherwise specified, Scripture quotations are taken from the New King James Version. © Copyright 1966 Holman bible Publishers Nashville, Tennessee. All Rights Reserved.

Text from NEW KING JAMES VERSION Copyright © 1982 by Thomas Nelson, Inc.

Verses marked NIV are taken from the HOLY BIBLE, NEW INTERNATIONAL VERSION. Copyright © 1973, 1978, 1984 by the International Bible Society. All rights reserved.

Verses marked NASB1995 are taken from the New American Standard Bible. Copyright © 1960, 1962, 1963, 1968, 1971, 1972, 1973, 1975, 1977, 1995 by the Lockman Foundation.

"The Potter and the Dizzy Clay," poem written by Faun Collett and illustrated by Debbie Jenkins, copyright 2020, all rights reserved. ISBN: 978-1-77359544-0-0

Scripture quotations marked net are taken from the NET Bible® copyright © 1996, 2019 by Biblical Studies Press, LLC. http://netbible.com. All rights reserved.

Scripture quotations marked (NASB) are taken from the New American Standard Bible, Copyright 1960, 1962, 1963, 1968, 1971, 1972, 1973, 1975, 1977, 1995 by The Lockman Foundation. Used by permission. (www.Lockman.org)

Scripture quotations marked (AMP) are taken from the Amplified Bible, Copyright 2015 by The Lockman Foundation. Used by permission. (www.Lockman.org.). All rights reserved.

Scripture quotations marked (AMPC) are taken from the Amplified Bible. Copyright 1954, 1958, 1962, 1964, 1965, 1987 by The Lockman Foundation. Used by permission. www.lockman.org.

The Jesus Whisperer
Copyright © 2022 Faun Collett
ISBN 978-1-949106-84-8

Published by Word and Spirit Publishing
P.O. Box 701403
Tulsa, Oklahoma 74170
wordandspiritpublishing.com

Printed in the United States of America. All rights reserved under International Copyright Law. Content and/or cover may not be reproduced in whole or in part in any form without the expressed written consent of the Publisher.

Dedication

I lovingly dedicate this book to those who have shared my journey for some distance. Our siblings, friends, and natural family members have richly blessed us, and our spiritual family has imparted a sense of belonging, acceptance, and devotion to community rarely found in this world. The gift of our beautiful grandchildren has filled our hopes with grandeur. May the hidden nuggets of eternity written on these pages inspire a heritage to serve God with word and deed.

And last but not least: I dedicate this book to Louie, Elvis, Jamie, Jon, Dana, Joe, little Missy Mae, Judy, Heather, Bryan, Todd, Melvin, Missy Mae, every child, youth, and adult, and countless others who graced our doorway at Faun-Haven and Amen-dogs, as well as the precious ones we have encountered through our church ministry in Florida. This book happened because of you. You are all deeply loved and a treasure in our lives. When you believe in Jesus Christ and receive Him as your Lord and Savior, everything changes.

Our testimony to overcome and our ability to rise above our circumstance was because of the love of God shed abroad in our hearts. The faithfulness of Jesus, the gentle guidance of the Holy Spirit, and the unfailing love of the Father has given us a quality of life and peace beyond what any eye can see. In John 16:33, Jesus said, "These things I have spoken to you, that in Me you may have peace. In the world you will have tribulation; but be of good cheer, I have overcome the world." I encourage every reader to seek out God, for He is the true Savior and Provider of peace during the storms of life.

A special thanks to my dear friend Maggie King. God answered my desperate cry and sent Maggie to set this book in order. She came day after day for months and labored tirelessly. When I think of her willingness to assist me with the organization of my book, I recall the words of Jesus, "The last will be first..." and her faithfulness has surpassed my greatest expectation. As an English teacher, her ability to compile, correct, and connect my writings for *The Jesus Whisperer* has been amazing. And her mentoring has been a priceless blessing.

Maggie, I am forever grateful and love you dearly.

Faun Collett, Author

Contents

Acknowledgements

First and foremost, I want to thank ABBA Father for the selfless gift of His Son, Jesus Christ! Jesus is sitting at His right hand making constant intercession for me, and the Holy Spirit is on earth now as the exact representation of Him—as my Comforter, Counselor, Mentor, and the Giver of gifts to empower me.

To my faithful partner, Douglas, who is the most remarkable man and husband a woman could ever have! He has filled my days with adventure and my nights with peace, contentment, and everlasting love. Your patience, encouragement, love, and devotion helped to motivate me. Our children have carried us the distance and infused within us a drive to leave a legacy of something more valuable than silver or gold. My son and daughter and their families, and Doug's children and their families, have all been arranged on our family tree. Paul wrote in 1 Thessalonians 4:16–17:

"For the Lord Himself will descend from heaven with a shout, with the voice of an archangel, and with the trumpet of God. And the dead in Christ will rise first. Then we who are alive and remain shall be caught up together with them in the clouds to meet the Lord in the air. And thus we shall always be with the Lord." I believe that one day we will all be gathered at our Father's heavenly table and live with our Lord forever.

My pastor in Missouri, Terry Roberts, and his beautiful wife, Becky, have been my dear friends and inspiration, equipping me with the uncompromised Word of God.

My Florida pastor, Alex Pappas, and his precious wife, Naomi, have encouraged me to press on to the goal, and they richly watered seeds of the fivefold ministry anointing where we are currently planted.

Margaret Thomas, Shirley Burrs, and my writer's guild, Treasure Coast Word Weavers, with their edits and critiques, all worked tirelessly, as if they had dropped down from heaven to help set everything in order. You are all loved beyond measure, and I am forever grateful for you.

Foreword

The author of *The Jesus Whisperer* is Faun Collett, a trusted and beloved friend of mine. I have never known a person who listened to God so intently, trusted Him so completely, and followed Him more closely. Daniel 11:32 states: *"The people who know their God will be strong and do great exploits!"* So it does not surprise me that Faun and her beloved husband, Doug, have been used so powerfully to transform the lives of 350 children both in and out of foster care, as well as so many other men and women over the last thirty-five years.

I have listened in wonder as Faun and Doug recount story after story of the work of the Holy Spirit in redeeming people who, as a clinical counselor, I would have feared were beyond hope because they were so broken. While it was being written, I read this book, *The Jesus Whisperer,* in several formats, and I deeply believe that Faun listens to the

Holy Spirit and has so much to teach the Body of Christ. I have noted throughout her life story that Faun has fine-tuned her heart to God so that what she says often seems to come straight from Jesus' lips to her ears. I have witnessed repeatedly in amazement as Faun wrote her amazing, inspirational poems while sitting right beside us in church as our pastor was preaching, and then later reading her poem or prose. The Holy Spirit seemed to directly dictate to Faun His words...word for word what she was to write...the theology and content in these poems was so cogent and profound! I maintain that either Faun is poetic prophet or a prophetic poet, who has a tremendous gift from the Holy Spirit. I have seen and heard Faun irresistibly minister to the broken and hurting with such passion and wisdom that they were swept into the love and life of God.

In this book, *The Jesus Whisperer*, Faun shares how she learned to really listen to the voice of God, to truly believe in His Word, and to immediately and courageously follow Jesus in whatever He is telling her to do. This is the secret of Faun's miraculous life and astounding life story...to simply listen to, trust, and obey God...faithfully in every season, despite the many challenges. I had asked Faun to share her story and reveal how she learned to be a Jesus whisperer, as I wanted to also enjoy such intimacy with Christ and have the Holy Spirit fill my life with similar miraculous encounters as she relates in this book.

In my personal devotions with God, I sing to Jesus a song I'm sure many of you know: *"Day by day, O dear Lord, three things I pray: To see You more clearly, follow You more nearly, to love You more dearly...day by day by day by day by day!"* It is my prayer that as you read Faun's book, *The Jesus Whisperer,* all these blessings will be your portion throughout your life. I hope Faun's book will help tune your spiritual ears to really hear Jesus and inspire you to begin to live a supernatural life filled with adventures in God!

> —**Rev. Dr. Kenneth N. Brown is a professional clinical counselor and psychotherapist** (D.MIN. M.DIV., DIP. O.P.C., B.SC, AAMFT).

A Word of Encouragement

Be filled with the Holy Spirit, learn about the armor of God, and study the Bible as if it were a letter written to you personally by the hand of God, because it truly is! May the "war room" in your "closet of prayer" equip you with a hope, future, and destiny, sealed with the signet ring of victory both now and forever.

Guided Scripture

To them God willed to make known what are the riches of the glory of this mystery among the Gentiles: which is Christ in you, the hope of glory.

—Colossians 1:27

Introduction
Whispering Hope

The Jesus Whisperer is a journey taken through seven decades of my life. As a lonely, misunderstood child, a teen in a failed marriage, a college student experiencing a nervous breakdown, and a young mother in a second failed marriage, I was hopeless, helpless, and defeated. After traversing valleys and mountaintops, in a moment of time, I finally heard that which had been there all along and I stepped into another dimension.

Suddenly the still, small voice became more distinctive than the louder voices of chaos and confusion bombarding my world. Then came a moment when the Whispering Hope of the Ages carried me back to familiar flashes of memory, and I finally began to see. He had always been with me, softly calling, gently guiding, patiently waiting for me to cross over from the natural to a supernatural destiny, my Promised Land. Come with me and see. We all suffer the same kinds of sorrows, but we don't all make it to the mountaintops. It takes recognizing a *Whisper* from the Holy Spirit to bring us to that place where we can finally connect and eventually qualify to become a *Jesus Whisperer.*

From natural methods to training under the supernatural Spirit of the living God, I discovered the truth. It is here that I was able to raise the dead, bring healing to the sick, and encourage the brokenhearted. *The Jesus Whisperer* will catapult anyone who hearkens to His voice into a power that few have experienced. This power is what enables us to be delivered, be set free, and thrive. God's Word is powerful and sharper than any "two-edged sword," rightly dividing truth in our innermost parts, and that truth can set anyone free. We are free by the wonderworking blood of the Lamb. There's a gift inside of you, placed there by your Maker, and that gift will make room for you.

You are the ones to whom Jesus is whispering, and I pray that His voice whispers into your future and motivates, equips, and inspires you with an even greater zeal and love for your King.

The *Jesus Whisperer* Prayer
God's Revelation to Elijah

Then a great and powerful wind tore the mountains apart and shattered the rocks before the LORD, but the LORD was not in the wind. After the wind there was an earthquake, but the LORD was not in the earthquake. After the earthquake came a fire...and after the fire came a gentle whisper.

—1 Kings 19:11–12 NIV

Father, I ask that You would help everyone reading this book to hear Your voice so we will not follow another voice, but only that of our Shepherd. Thank You for the privilege we have

while we take to heart Your instructions to meditate upon Your holy Word. We especially give thanks to the Holy Spirit as He counsels, guides, and empowers us to comprehend the mysteries of the Kingdom.

Give each of us ears to hear what Your Spirit is saying to everyone who picks up this book. Help us apply that Word to our lives in a real and practical way as we walk out our destiny with You. I'm asking that You impart a supernatural message that will equip us to fulfill Your call on all our lives as we seek Your face and incline our ears to Your Word. Holy Spirit, I invite You to fill this short time with instruction and inspiration, to help us hear Your voice and to do Your bidding. In Jesus' name, amen.

Emmanuel Whispers

Emmanuel whispers His purpose and plans

to ears who will hear His call.

Emmanuel whispers His joys and cares

to those who seek His all.

Emmanuel whispers to every heart

that responds to His gentle refrain.

Emmanuel whispers, and when He does,

I listen and praise His holy name.

Chapter 1

Reflections on a Journey with My Heavenly Father

Even a child is known by his deeds, whether what he does is pure and right.

—Proverbs 20:11 NKJV

My parents had a profound influence on my young life as I progressed from my childhood to my teenage years and eventually adulthood. I view my family as one of God's formative gifts, for it is with them that my need for our heavenly Father was established, and for that, I am continually thankful.

Faith-Driven Cultural Influences

Music was a priority in my household and an opportunity for family bonding. My mother and father worked very hard to make ends meet, and it took a toll on both of them. Mom tried her best to teach my sisters and me to be modest, polite, proper, and well-behaved. Fashion was important to her, and she dressed her girls like royalty, but she paid a heavy price because she had to make much of our clothing, especially for special occasions like Easter, Thanksgiving, and Christmas.

She had a creative flair and loved decorating. She specialized in making something out of the ordinary, like gluing material on the walls because she could not afford wallpaper, or sewing carpet squares together to make our rugs, all while working full-time and still coming home to fix a family dinner before tending to the house. She was only four-foot-eleven, but she took on the world with all the gusto she could muster, along with a powerful faith that helped pull us all through some pretty rough circumstances.

Going to church was important to her, and many times she would dress us to the hilt and walk several blocks to the nearest bus stop with a baby in her arms and my sister and me hand in hand. Going to church on a Sunday morning, then returning to prepare our Sunday dinner, was an overwhelming agenda, but she never complained. Motherhood was difficult, but she loved her girls and wanted the best for us. Through nursing my middle sister back to health after many sleepless nights at the hospital, she stayed by her side during my sister's heart surgery and recovery at four years old; to taking me to Shriner's Hospital for spinal taps and treatments for curvature of the spine; to handling the cancer treatments of my younger sister, Mom was always faithfully and prayerfully by our side and trusting God for His divine intervention. I wrote the following poem for her on Mother's Day as a tribute to her love.

Mother

I've never faced a challenge
Like the one I'm facing now,
To put in words a tribute
To my mother, tell me how.

She's been more than maternal,
My counselor and my friend.
She's been my inspiration,
And her love will never end.

To really do her justice,
I would have to travel time
Through almost half a century
Of her life poured into mine.

The first things I remember
Are the nursery rhymes she read,
And all the drawn-out prayers she heard
Before I went to bed.

And I recall the shopping trips
With a harness wrapped around me.
She'd lead me on a leash through stores
While people watched profoundly.

I think about the moments
When she had so much to do,
But she always stopped and took the time
To work my problems through.

She always had advice to give:
"Stand straight and practice hygiene;
"Be careful and be prayerful;
"Mind your manners, God is watching."

There never seemed to be an end
To the counsel I had heard.
She helped me live for others
And prepared me with God's Word.

The Bible speaks that wisdom starts
By a deep respect for God;
That spoiled children happen
With the sparing of the rod.

Well, I know the rod was spared some,
And I got by with quite a bit,
But the lessons that I learned from Mom
Were embellished with her wit.

As I began to leave behind
Those careless childhood days,
I faced the challenge of this world
Equipped with Mother's praise.

It's awesome when I contemplate
Her worthiness alone.
She holds a place exalted
When my thoughts are turned to home.

If home is where the heart is,
There's a room that's like no other,
A royal chamber filled with love
For my precious, priceless mother.

by Faun Collett

This small tribute to my mother's devotion and her love for all of us is just a glimpse of her dedication to her children and family. She loved God and did everything she knew to do to instill the love of Jesus into the hearts of her family. She emphasized tithing and giving, teaching us that we can never outgive God and that we should take care of His house first. God gave His first and His best, and giving to Him was the best thing we could do with our money.

Mom lived until her eightieth birthday, and we had a birthday party in her hospital room. Although Mother had developed a staph infection (MERSA) at the hospital and was too weak to fight it off, she wasn't about to miss her party. Unable to eat, but motioning for doctors, nurses, and hospital employees to have some cake, her gift of hospitality welcomed all. Everybody loved her, and her three girls, grandchildren, and her brother, Jack, all gathered around her bed for one last farewell shortly before she went home to be with the Lord. The following year, on Mom's birthday, I wrote this poem.

Mom's First Birthday in Heaven

To all my loved ones, may this message
Cause your hearts to smile.
A special day has traveled by
To stay with us awhile.

Though it may only last as long
As any other day,
The memories that it brings to us
Will never go away.
For February twenty-fourth
Reminds us once again
How very blessed and cherished
All of us have been.

It floods our minds with antics
of her endless tender care
And all the precious moments
That our family had to share.

Our tender friend and grandma,
Our treasured, priceless mother,
What greater present can we give
Than to celebrate each other?

So, on this happy birthday,
let's bow our hearts in prayer,
Thank God we have each other,
And know she's waiting for us there!

Dear Lord, would You please tell her,
We're all safe and doing fine?
Happy, happy birthday, Momma,
We're lovin' ya all the time!

by Faun Collett

A mother is a precious gift from God, and a godly mother who lovingly teaches and guides her children in a moral and God-fearing manner is a blessing to her children throughout their lives.

Dad: A Gift from the Heavenly Father

Dad was the one who took the time to work with my sisters and me in music appreciation. His patience paid off, because it wasn't long before we were all singing our parts in harmony while I strummed on the little Martin Ukulele or Tenor Guitar that he taught me to play. Because of his love of music and singing, he taught his children the joy and love of music. My sisters and I had a special and unique blending when we sang that families sometimes exhibit. Several times we had opportunities to entertain at events like amateur nights. *Stan Kann Amateur Hour* was a television show that wanted us to audition, but Dad didn't want his girls in show business. He was concerned because of the rough crowds and wrong kinds of influence that could threaten our innocence, so we had to be satisfied with just our little family gatherings, times that were written on our hearts forever.

Dad's voice was extraordinary, as well as the wealth of back home songs he had stored in his heart for our fun and lighthearted times together. As a young man, he was multi-talented and played a trumpet in the big bands. He taught ballroom dance lessons for Arthur Murray Studios, and he took us all on amazing excursions from time to time on the St. Louis USS *Admiral.*

Perhaps the most memorable characteristic of my father was the love and patriotism he openly displayed for his country and how proud he was to have served in the U.S. Navy during World War II. Every year, from the time the war ended until the year Dad died, his squadron would come together from all over the United States and renew old friendships. His fellow squadron members would laugh and cut up with exaggerated stories and hilarious jokes as they reflected on years gone by. They were proud of their country and devoted to each other, and no history class on earth could compete with the awesome patriotic legacy they left behind. They would laugh, love, and sing until the wee hours of the morning. The song I remember the most was called "Over There."

Later in life, Dad was diagnosed with emphysema, and when he began coughing excessively, we knew his time on earth was dwindling. On his eightieth birthday, I began to shop for a present that would be special to him. I walked into a memorabilia shop and happened upon a very old picture of a consolidated PBY Catalina that dad flew on during the war. He was an engineer and had to keep his ship in tiptop condition, but that job was a huge undertaking because the big boat of a plane was designed to carry heavy cargo like bombs, machinery, artillery, tanks, and vehicles overseas to destinations that were dangerous and weighty.

The PBY was a complex plane because it was designed for multiple tasks, as well as landing on both water and land. Although the PBY was necessary to the war cause, it was also the most unstable and known for its frequent malfunctions. On one particular day, Dad's squadron was to take a test run at his naval base, and everyone, including Dad, loaded onto the plane. At the last minute, Dad was called back to the office to fill out some kind of paperwork. Shortly after he left the plane, it took off, and Dad looked back to see a tremendous explosion in the air. He later was told the plane had crashed and everybody on board was lost. It was a devastating and extremely emotional time for him, one that I don't think he ever really got over. However, it did give him a renewed perspective of his destiny, and his faith in God became deeper through that experience.

Dad joined the Navy choir, with one of his favorite songs being **"Steal away to Jesus."** He sang it often to me, and I loved hearing him sing. It has become one of my favorite songs, as well, but when Dad would gather with his Navy buddies, they always sang "Over There." When I found the original score next to that picture of the PBY, I had them both framed, as well as the following poem I wrote for him called "Over There."

Over There

The antique paper shop looked bare
as I began to browse around,
And the memorabilia lured me to a picture I had found.
For years it sat and waited until I came along,
And when I picked it up, Dad, I heard this Navy song.

I didn't hear it with my ears, yet deep inside of me,
I heard this song of sailors in triumphant jubilee.
The song was sung on land and sea, the song was in the air,
With thoughts toward home and victory, those boys sang
"Over There."

It took me back to World War II,
when your squadron won the war,
With love and pride and thankfulness,
I knew who you won it for.
And I'm sure, Dad, I was with you when you flew that PBY,
Though way back then, I was not much more
than a twinkle in your eye.

Now, half a century later, you've given me your best,
And, Dad, I know you're tired, and someday soon you'll rest.
But when that battle rages here, I'll be with you in a prayer,
And we'll always be together, Dad, forever "Over There."

Inspired by the love of God and country,
Faun Collett

During Dad's last few days, our family witnessed a level of hospital care and special attention given to him at every shift change that was astonishing. When the hospital staff would change his sheets, our family would observe an unusual habit as they tied knots in his sheets at the foot of his bed. After several nights, curiosity overtook us, and we finally asked why the knots were there. We were lovingly told that patients with knots in their sheets signaled the next shift of caregivers to take extra care because they were very special. That summed up my dad better than anything else I could say. The following poem I wrote three years later, when my father finally crossed over into heaven.

He Loves Me Knot, He Loves Me

A boy tied a knot in his new duffel bag
With all that he owned in his sack.
Leaving his family and old hometown,
He threw his bag over his back.

Holding on tight with the knot he had made,
While wrapping it over his hand,
He bravely signed up to serve in the war,
And the boy came back as a man.

He was young and strong, and the knot held long,
Securing all he held dear.
A sailor is proud of the knots he can tie,
And he uses them year after year.

He knew his knots, and some folks say
He was in knots on his wedding day.
After the wedding, with his beautiful bride,
He was sure it's the best knot that he ever tied.

Soon there were little ones filling their home,
Learning to tie little knots of their own.
He loved them and taught them each knot that they knew,
Amazed at how quickly his little ones grew.

His days turned to years,
Then his years into sand,
And as strange as it seems,
He was now an old man.

We all stood around his hospital room,
Not knowing what we would do.
He had bound us together as no one else could
And had always carried us through.

We were still in his room,
Overwhelmed with our grief,
When the nurses began
Tying knots in his sheets.

When we finally asked
Why the knots were tied there,
They said it's a code
To give more tender care.

The patients they find
With knots at their feet
Will signal he's special.
Take good care of him, please.

We knew it was time to release his sweet soul.
His time here was nearing the end.
Through all he had shared and imparted to us,
We were losing much more than a friend.

Silent tears that we cried as we stood by his side
Were only a sign of our pain.
Letting him go was the best we could do;
We knew that our loss was his gain.

For Dad still had a journey to make,
With love his greatest reward.
We knew we would join him again before long
To unite with our King and our Lord.

And though he was slowly slipping away,
The knots were reminders of the love that will stay.
His legacy wasn't in the tears that we cried,
But the Love Knots Dad had tied when he died.

Inspired by a Loving Father,
Faun Collett

As I reflect on my father's memory, I am reminded of a Bible verse about God's gifts from heaven: "Every good gift and every perfect gift is from above, and comes down from the Father of lights, with whom there is no variation or shadow of turning" (James. 1:17). For me, the most valuable gifts that God has given me are my salvation and my future home in heaven. The Scriptures tell us, "But seek first the kingdom of God and His righteousness, and all these things shall be added to you" (Matthew 6:33). So, I encourage you to reach out to God and enthusiastically follow Him, and He will provide for you, just like He has for me. From the time I was born and throughout my adult life, God has always worked miracles in my life, even when the challenges seemed hopeless. He was there—always there—just waiting to *whisper* His words and blessings into my life.

On a Personal Journey to Meet My Heavenly Father

After I was born and released from the hospital, my parents took me to my first home, which was a small apartment on the second floor near downtown St. Louis, on a street called Compton. There are family pictures that show my parents and their best friends posing on the steps of our apartment as they prepared to carry me over the threshold of my early childhood. I've been told that money was scarce after World War II, and in August 1946, I was one of the first Baby Boomers to make her debut. My dad's friend had to get me out of hock by paying the hospital bill before they could bring me home. That was the beginning of my (MO) legacy, of being rescued all my life.

The earliest memories I have are when I was four years old and running barefoot in our little fenced-in back yard, next to the alley that followed several brick buildings to a huge, bigger-than-life two-story ice-cream cone in front of Velvet Freeze. I was completely blindsided by a bumblebee who protested being run over by a barefoot little girl, and the bumblebee rejected my intrusion into its world by leaving its stinger in my foot. My father, hearing my screams of terror, ran down a flight of steps, scooped me up, and after pulling the stinger out, consoled me with a big hug. He set me on his shoulders for a short jog to indulge me with a double-dip orange-sherbet cone, and all the pain quickly went away.

During this time of my life, I remember making mudpies underneath the porch steps with my little playmate Johnny, who helped me celebrate the birth of my new baby sister, Carla Sue, as she was carried across the same threshold as I was four years earlier. It seemed to be the beginning of an exciting, new adventure, and for the most part, it was. I was so young then, but I did understand that Carla was not a healthy child because she was born with a heart problem that would later require surgery. Carla required a lot of Mom's attention, and for a young child to understand the severity of Carla's situation was impossible. However, as I grew in age, I did realize there were dire situations that had to be addressed concerning Carla's future health. Later in life, I wrote a poem that sums up my feelings of Carla with a fair amount of accuracy.

Carla Sue

It seems not all so long ago, that I was making pies
Beneath the porch on Compton Street, preparing a surprise.
My little playmate Johnny and my dolly, Suzie-Q,
Had gathered for a baby shower for newborn Carla Sue.

The mudpies were delicious, and the tea was poured with care,
While we welcomed my new sister
and pretended she was there.
Well, that was only make-believe,
and your arrival seemed like fun,
Until reality set in—I was no longer number one!

At first your bottle feedings gave me something fun to do,
As I was Momma's helper, and we coddled over you.
But then, the changing diapers, the baths, and constant care,
The oohs and goos and cries and smiles,
the fuss over your red hair.

It began to shed a different light on your precious angel face.
This new center of attention was invading all my space.
Now, I was only four years old when I began to get the picture.
There weren't much room in my small world
for a red-haired baby sister.

Things didn't get much better as you sweetly grew in grace.
First smile, first foods, first steps, first words,
and I was second place.
So, when the family gathered, it was very plain to see
That you were very special to everyone BUT ME!

Don't get me wrong, 'cause from the start,
I knew I was no match
For this brown-eyed, red-haired wonder,
our family's Cabbage Patch.
She mesmerized us with her rare ability to chatter,
And play the grown-up part, as if her young age didn't matter.

It's funny how, at four years old, you didn't miss a trick.
Not very much got past you, though you were very sick.
You see, our family sheltered me, and I never saw the death
That stalked your frail, thin body
with each labored, shallow breath.

No wonder all that fuss was made from Daddy's pregnant wife.
My precious baby sister was bravely fighting for her life.
At four years old, no longer could the doctors stall your fate.
Your little heart required repair, they had to operate.

I remember well that fateful day; I think I was but seven.
With a tearstained face, I begged the Lord,
"PLEASE, don't take my sis to heaven!
"I know that I've been mean to her, but if You let her stay,
"I'll tell her stories and give her love
and include her when I play."

And so sincere, my humble plea was heard from God above,
For all of us had cried that prayer,
you were returned to us to love.
And loved you were with grateful hearts,
we laughed when you were pesky.
You grew each day with vim and vigor,
and soon you got quite testy.

And I forgot that special promise I had made to God the Father.
Now, you'd have to learn my stories
if my play you would not bother.
And somehow, I began to notice things got out of hand.
It seemed each time I turned around you needed a reprimand.

And so, I took it upon myself to raise you right for Mother.
After all, her schedule stretched to soon include another.
She wouldn't let me spank you, so I was pushed to yellin'.
The only leverage that I had was to threaten I was tellin'.

The truth is, it was hard to find a flaw in your sweet nature.
When I was stern, you'd find a way to soften and to nurture.
You seemed to be in awe of me and thought it was a treat
When I'd make up little stories, and you'd listen at my feet.

You'd beg me for attention and persistently pursued
To follow me, and covet me, though I acted mad and rude.
And though you seemed an aggravation,
I remember special times
Of peace and sweet contentment of a friendship so sublime.

How we huddled in the winter on a register of heat
And snuggled on the bathroom floor,
where we would warm our feet.
We'd laugh and wile away the hours to play some silly things,
And when we had to do the dishes, we'd often start to sing.

So, singing became a way of life that gave our family pleasure.
After supper in the evening, we'd all gather with this treasure.
By now, that new addition, our younger sister, Kim,
Began to sing and harmonize, and Dad taught us all a hymn.

"Hear our prayer, O Lord," we'd sing to our hearts' release,
"Incline Thine ear to us, and grant to us Thy peace."
Dear precious sister Carla, God has granted our petition,
For your value can't be measured when I go to reminiscin'.

Our childhood paved a way for us that only made us better.
While growing up we formed a bond
that kept us strong together.
Through all these years, the riches that you have given me
Are protected in the memories of your precious legacy.

Inspired by a Gift from God,
Faun Collett

With Change, God Introduces Challenges in Life

In life, there are many challenges, and many of those difficulties start in childhood. Sometimes the challenges involve inner insecurities that are beyond the control of a child, but they can have negative effects on a person's emotional and spiritual development. As parents, we have the responsibility to teach our children that we are God-centered, and we should instill in them that they should be God-centered as well. In the book of Isaiah, God's Word reveals that: "Even youths grow tired and weary, and young men stumble and fall; but those who hope in the Lord will renew their strength. They will soar on wings like eagles; they will run and not grow weary, they will walk and not be faint" (Isaiah 40:30–31 niv). My parents taught me the importance of faith in God, and I am very thankful for them, because they set the foundation for my need to accept God into my life. I learned early on in life that I needed God's blessings to protect my parents and my siblings, as well as His forgiveness, when I was disappointed from the small disillusionments in life.

Shortly after Carla's surgery, and before the dust settled from all the commotion, my mother delivered our next sibling. She already had two girls, and her close friends seemed convinced that a boy was in order. Back in the 1950s, it was always a guessing game—some people believed that if a mother carried the baby out front, it would be a boy, but if she carried it in an oblong manner, it was a girl. Needless to say, our little family was expecting a boy and we had his name already picked out, so when "he" turned out to be a "she," my world was crushed. It's strange how family members can experience life from different perspectives. Unfortunately, Kimmy was always told that I cried when she was born and that I was disappointed she was a girl. Growing up in the same household can leave a lasting impression on a child who is eight years younger and always getting in the way. It didn't take a rocket scientist to figure out that Kimmy didn't think I loved her, but nothing could be further from the truth. Although she didn't tell me how she felt until she was much older, I was brokenhearted that she carried those feelings the whole time she was growing up; so I wrote the following poem for her when she turned thirty years old:

Unexpected Joy

Kim, when I was only eight years old,
I remember watching Mother.
Excitement built as she came due
To have my baby brother.

So many thoughts and prayers went out
And daydreams filled with joy.
I couldn't wait till Mama had
Our little baby boy.

In the first week of November
Of nineteen fifty-four,
Mama had a nosebleed,
And they rushed her out the door.

Chaos filled the household,
My head was in a whirl,
And on November fifth I learned
My brother was a girl.

I cried with disappointment;
My heart was filled with gloom,
Until at last they brought you home
And took you to my room.

I think the very moment
That I saw you with my eyes,
The disappointment left me,
And I smiled at my surprise.

So tiny and so beautiful
In a bassinet of white,
The wonderment of seeing you
Was precious in my sight.

Though I was young and really thought
You should have been a mister,
I bowed my head and thanked the Lord
For my little baby sister.

Now the span of years between us
Hindered sharing childhood things,
But being sisters has a way
Of filling voids with dreams.

Dreams about our future
That only sisters share,
Through good and bad, our hearts are bound
With tender loving care.

I love you, Kim, happy birthday!

Inspired by sisterly love,
Faun Collett

As I reflect on Kim's birth and childhood challenges, I am reminded of how her childhood beginnings and struggles in life affected me, as well. I wanted a baby brother, but God gave us the most beautiful baby girl. God had a purpose for Kim, just as He has a purpose for you. He did not give up on Kim, and He will not give up on you.

When Kim was preschool age, she could sing every word of any song she ever heard. I knew she had a good mind and a great memory, but when she went into grade school, learning became a challenge. My parents took her to a doctor, who diagnosed her with dyslexia. There were no treatment plans for that disability at that time, and she struggled all the way through school. Later in life, she met and married a young man whom we welcomed into our family. She worked to help put him through culinary school, and he became a fine chef. In her early twenties, she had some female complications that would lead to great disappointments in her life. After she went through various medical tests, the results revealed she had stage-four uterine cancer. Her doctor suggested packing her with radium and indicated she didn't have long to live.

Our family was devastated. I belonged to a Christian group called Day Spring, and one of the members was an ob-gyn. I asked him if he would go the hospital and pray for her. He went the next day and felt he should consult with a doctor who was known as a successful cancer surgeon. Upon examination, he said he believed he could do a radical operation that would give her a longer lifespan. The surgery went flawlessly, and Kim has now been cancer-free for over fifty years. We knew God had answered our prayers, but Kimmy would never be able to bear children. Her husband said he wanted children and filed for divorce. Her body healed, but her heart was broken. Eventually Kim took an interest in ambulance work and studied to be a paramedic. That accomplishment was monumental in her life. Her vibrant personality and caring nature helped her transition into a business venture with her new husband, and shortly after that, they adopted a son, Dustin.

Personal Challenges and God's Safety Net

During my own childhood, I, too, would face challenges that would test my strength and willingness to choose to fight, but that would also force me to seek a spiritual relationship with my heavenly Father. My childhood days were filled with rejection. I was the only girl in my class through the six years of elementary school. The *only girl,* in a class full of boys who made a daily practice of teasing and taunting me. The upper-grade girls distanced themselves from me because hairstyles, makeup, fashion, and boys were their primary interests, and the younger girls were too childish, so I played by myself. I was bullied relentlessly, and insecurities began to build. I was always the last one chosen for team sports, excluded during playground activities, and made fun of constantly—these were daily events in my life. Even the little things other kids did, like lifting up my ponytail and saying, "I always wanted to see what was under a pony's tail," would bring me to tears. *Self-consciousness and doubt plagued me.*

Sitting out team selections was trying from the playground at school to the large empty lot at the bottom of Ripple Street. Neighborhood kids gathered on weekends at the bottom of our hill to play ball. *Pick me, pick me,* was always the cry of my heart, but nobody ever did. This set the stage for my feelings of insecurity, which carried well into my future. It felt like nobody liked me, and so I decided I didn't like myself. Locking myself into a make-believe world reinforced my isolation, but that is where I felt safe. Entertaining myself developed my creativity in play as I exercised my imagination. During this season of life "make-believe" was something I learned to do very well. These extenuating circumstances pulled me into a sweet, fun, wonderful world of fantasy. Climbing trees, catching snakes and lizards, playing with kittens or dogs, and exploring my backyard filled many lonely hours, and I read comic books by the dozens.

Night after night, Mom would read Mother Goose stories and poetry books to me and talk to me about Jesus. This was my safe haven, and it is there where I was sensitized to the quiet *whispers* of our heavenly Father.

With change come challenges in a child's life, and the presence of God is essential for the development of emotional and spiritual stability. I loved God from my earliest memories, and hearing His voice was always comforting to me. We attended a small neighborhood church, where Sunday school teachers Fred and Virginia had a tremendous impact on me. Their teachings about Jesus touched my world in a profound and powerful way. Every day brought a closer walk with Jesus, and every night as I knelt beside my bed, I would pray, "Now I lay me down to sleep. I pray the Lord my soul to keep. If I should die before I wake, I pray the Lord my soul to take. Bless my family and everyone else in the whole wide world, amen." Feeling deeply loved by Jesus gave me great comfort. Reading the Bible as a child was not encouraged, yet His living Word was alive in me.

As I reflect on this portion of my life's journey, I realize that rejection can be traumatizing, especially for a child who feels there is no acceptance for his or her presence. Children do not have the social or emotional skills to deal with rejection, and unfortunately, far too many adults struggle with it as well. When I was a child, I allowed rejection to define me, but as I grew in age and faith, I realized that the possibilities for my life were endless, and that God had a purpose for me. I realize now that God had a plan all along for me. My struggles would lead me to better things in life and prepare me to serve the Lord and fulfill my own destiny. In the book of Psalms, God says, "I will instruct you and teach you in the way you should go; I will guide you with My eye" (Psalm 32:8). I encourage you to seek our heavenly Father, lean on Him, and let Him guide you through this earthly life, because he will be your saving grace.

Spiritual Journey

When I was eight, my third-grade teacher taught us about poetry. When she gave us the assignment to turn in our first poem, I heard God *whisper* the words to me. I remember it to this day.

He Whispered

The Lord made the people and the animals, too,
And God made me, just as He made you.
He sent His Son down from heaven above,
To teach us about Him and to teach us of love.

He died on the cross to save us from sin,
Then let us live freely, both women and men.
So, this I tell you, how the world did begin,
All because of the Lord and His Son helping Him.

by Faun Collett

After the assignment was turned in, my teacher sent a letter home to my mom, saying the poem was too good. She thought I must have copied it from somewhere, and she gave me a failing grade. I was crushed and began to withdraw because of the further rejection and lack of trust. Fortunately, during my teen years, the Holy Spirit began to console me with two beautiful hymns.

Whispering Hope

There were two songs that I loved as a child. One was "Whispering Hope":

Soft as the voice of an angel,
Breathing a lesson unheard,
Hope with a gentle persuasion
Whispers her comforting word:

Wait till the darkness is over,
Wait till the tempest is done,
Hope for the sunshine tomorrow,
After the shower is gone.

Refrain:
Whispering hope, oh how welcome thy voice,
Making my heart in its sorrow rejoice.

In the Garden

I come to the garden alone,

While the dew is still on the roses,

And the voice I hear falling on my ear

The Son of God discloses

And He walks with me

And He talks with me

And He tells me I am His own

And the joy we share as we tarry there

None other has ever known.

The music brought a gentle peace to my heart, and deep inside I began to awaken to His presence. Although I felt lonely, His gentle calling helped me to realize I wasn't as alone as it seemed. A little here, a little there, His *whispers* rose inside my spirit, and I began to hear Him speak to me. Hearing His voice is one of the greatest joys I have ever known.

God's Amazing Gifts Are Also Found in His Creatures

Although my childhood was afflicted with emotional issues, our heavenly Father provided me with gifts that filled empty corners with music and fur babies. My parents moved when I was going into the first grade. They began to rent a house owned by my great-aunt and great-uncle in historical Dog Town, St. Louis. We lived on Ripple Street at the top of a steep hill. At the bottom of the hill were some of the last signs of the rural lifestyle merging into the city. Uncle Jim was not our blood uncle, but he carried the name the neighbors affectionately called him. He had a little plot of land with the flavor of country living.

On the edge of the city limits, he raised chickens, goats, kittens, a few dogs, and a horse named Dandy. He had the sweetest little honey-colored dog named Honey-Gal. In my heart, she belonged to me along with a mutt named Old Tex. The dogs were free to roam throughout the neighborhoods, and they enjoyed food scraps tossed from leftover meals. Together with some strays, they followed me everywhere I went.

At eight years old, I was the leader of a pack consisting of at least four to eight canines and bonding with every dog within a five-mile radius. Before school in the morning, these dogs would meet me in my yard, then walk with me several blocks to the corner, watching me turn toward school. I would command them to stay on the corner. Allowing them to follow any closer to the school grounds would have risked them being caught by the dog catchers. Every day after school, my little pack would join me, meeting on the same corner to walk back home. Somehow they knew what time school let out, and they would faithfully assemble in the afternoon.

Without realizing it, I became the neighborhood dog whisperer. My father's observations on animal behavior carried over from being raised on a farm. His responsibilities working with different animals had sparked his love of and interest in nature. With Dad passing on helpful information, dog training was easy for me. When he took me to adopt my first puppy from the Humane Society, it was love at first sight, and I named him Champ. Every free moment I had was taken up with this little champion, and together we won first place in the Oakland Playground Dog Show. A blue ribbon with this little German shepherd/beagle mix might as well have been made of gold. My confidence began to grow. Dogtown was the perfect spot for a lonely child who loved animals.

During my elementary school years, I yearned to escape to the country. Every summer, I'd beg Mom and Dad to let me stay on a farm. Dear friends who had stood up for them at their wedding lived on a large farm in Illinois. I was invited to stay with them for a few weeks when school let out. Finally, my dream had come true. Outfitted with my own bib overalls, my excitement could barely be contained. I got to do it all! Life on the farm was busy, as I collected eggs, milked cows, and churned butter. There was farm work from daybreak to nightfall, but I was allowed time to enjoy the animals. Riding the horses and playing in the barn with newborn kittens and puppies was better than I had imagined. I felt like I was in heaven. These experiences helped mold me into the person I am today. In addition, they helped me see all of God's creations as gifts from our heavenly Father.

God's Hand in Guiding Change

As the years passed in my young life, my old phonograph became a solace that ushered in my teenage years. I spent countless hours listening to classical music. Every instrument in the orchestra came alive as concert sounds filled my room. Beautiful scenes of nature entered my imagination as I closed my eyes to envision them. One night in my dreams, I composed an entire philharmonic score, with all of the instruments blending their sounds together. When I woke up, I cried because I didn't know how to write down what I had composed.

This inspired my mom to send me to Washington University to take music appreciation classes, but it was difficult for me to understand. Dad likely saw melancholy changes in my temperament and countered the sadness with his love for nature and music. While whistling or singing a cheery tune, he would point to trees, flowers, and birds and share intriguing facts. His humor, music, and love of nature stayed with me far beyond the days of my youth.

My parents did everything they could do to give my sisters and me a wonder-filled childhood. From Christmas presents, birthday gifts, room decorations, and allowances, I can't remember lacking anything. I was entrusted with freedoms few children were allowed. The rules were basic: Let someone know where you are going and be back before dark. There were few limitations or boundaries for one so young, and the places available for discovery were amazing. I ventured to museums, arena events, the Highlands, and Forest Park sites on foot and by bus or streetcar. My education outside of school built my self-confidence, but even at that age, I still realized there was something missing in my life.

Teen Challenges

It is crucial in the lives of teens that the Word of God is taught and felt in the inner circle of a family. Our God has a purpose for each of us. Children need to be taught early on that God has a plan for them and will lead them to their destiny. Scientists have discovered that a child's brain is not completely formed until he or she reaches the ages of eighteen to twenty-one. *Therefore, the fruit of the Spirit needs to be reinforced throughout a child's life.* The New Testament tells us, "And He has made from one blood every nation of men to dwell on all the face of the earth, and has determined their preappointed times and the boundaries of their dwellings" (Acts 17:26). The Bible says that God establishes our boundaries, but I sure didn't understand at that time that I was exactly where I should be.

In ninth grade, I joined the Mariner Girl Scouts, and I stayed in the group all the way through high school. The other scouts were the only friends I had, and we mustered up more adventure-filled fun than most kids ever have. We went on float trips in canoes, and sailing, swimming, camping, and cookouts along with Mariner land and sea events gave us awesome opportunities to develop our skills, including Morse code, charts and navigation, the rules of the road, and knots and splicing. This prepared us for yearly meets at the GAM (a German word for "games"). Girls from all over the United States gathered every year for two weeks at Sunnen Lake in Potosi, Missouri, to see who would take home the honor of top ship of the year. Our ship was the *Savannah.* We usually took home the most ribbons, and we cherished the friendships we made as we learned how to work as a team.

I was allowed to bring my musical instruments to camp. The lessons Dad gave me throughout the year helped build my confidence to play for the groups we entertained at home. So gathering around a bonfire with other campers came naturally, and our music filled the night air. It felt as if I had finally found my place, and I began to bond with my lifelong friends from the Mariners.

Those star-studded nights with the crackling campfire, tree frogs singing with the whippoorwills, and the fresh, crisp night air was the foundation for me to seek the Creator, who had gifted the world with such splendor. I believed, and I wanted to know all about Him. I had been raised in church, and I'd heard wonderful stories most of my young life about Jesus. Summer Bible camp, vacation Bible school, and Christian skits testified of His love. Enduring songs, singing in the choir, and attending Sunday school magnified everything about Him, but I didn't know Him for myself. I wrote about Him, but I still didn't know Him. If I had told you all about my father, showed you pictures, sang songs about him, and daily shared with you the most precious family times involving my father, you'd know a lot about my father, but you wouldn't know him until you encountered him for yourself. It is the same way with Jesus; you must want to know Him for yourself and accept Him into your life. I encourage you to do so, because I want you to be part of my heavenly Father's family.

Thus, that is the way my journey began with God. I was infatuated with Jesus, but it wasn't until I was a teenager at church camp that I began to search for the truth, and sadly enough, I realized that religion did not give me what I needed. I pray that you search for Him, too, and build a close personal *relationship* with Him that becomes more to you than just a religion.

A Seasons of Change

When I was eighteen, I married a young man who was no more prepared to be a husband than I was to be a wife. Unfortunately, our marriage ended after three months, and my life changed in a dramatic way. Shortly after my divorce, I began a journey of rebellion and exploration that took me to places and events that would influence my life in a negative way, yet they would eventually bring back to my heavenly Father.

In the fall of 1965, when I was nineteen, I decided to go away to college at Southeast Missouri State University in Cape Girardeau. I majored in physical education and minored in child psychology. Through the next decade of my life, I found what most young people long to discover: freedom! Freedom to see who I wanted, stay out late, stay up late, study when I felt like it, cut classes if I wanted to, and explore the college life of *"I did it my way!"* I smoked and cussed. I held down two jobs and carried over seventeen credit hours. My first job was at the Sabine House, where I lived off campus. Mrs. Sabine let me work in the kitchen, helping to prepare and serve meals, then clean up. After classes, I went to work at an all-night steakhouse, clocking in from 8 p.m. until 8 a.m., six nights a week.

All of that work didn't give me much time to study, although during slow times the restaurant manager would let me sit in a booth and get some reading in. Nonetheless, I loved college. The classes were interesting, and campus life was a life of its own. I spent any free time I could find between classes at the Marquette Newman Center playing Ping-Pong; I became the Ping-Pong champion of the center in no time. I began to forget my past, especially when I met a young photographer who had grown up in Webster Groves. We hit it off great until he wanted me to "come into the dark room and see what developed." I wanted no part of that and stuck more to my studies.

During the next summer break, I went to work for the YMCA summer camp for two years as a counselor to help fund my college tuition. I learned a lot about leadership during those summer days, and I came back to college with more zeal than ever. I never dreamed my grandchildren would one day experience camping at a YMCA camp many years later. God was definitely put on the back burner at that time. It was the late sixties, the era of the flower child, the "make love, not war" generation. Students would spray-paint bedsheets with huge letters that read, "God is dead," and hang them out of their dorm windows. That made me mad, and even though I wasn't serving Him, I got a bumper sticker for my car that read, *"MY GOD IS NOT DEAD— SORRY ABOUT YOURS."*

Later, I would realize that my life was no more than an empty vessel without God, and for me to ever find happiness, I had to build a *relationship* with God that would grow and sustain me through the rest of my life—not just for a season.

Prayer

Heavenly Father, I beseech You to give our readers ears to hear, eyes to see, and a heart to understand Your call and divine will for their lives. Give them the unction by Your Holy Spirit to seek You and overcome the mountains the enemy would try to put in their way. Supernaturally strengthen them to press on with endurance and perseverance. Assure them they are Your beloved child and that You will incline their ear to You as they seek You with all their hearts. Amen.

Notes

Notes

Chapter 2

Relationships

Then [the LORD] said, "Go out, and stand on the mountain before the LORD." And behold, the LORD passed by, and a great and strong wind tore into the mountains and broke the rocks in pieces before the LORD, but the LORD was not in the wind, and after the wind an earthquake, but the LORD was not in the earthquake, and after the earthquake a fire...and after the fire came [the *whisper*].

—1 Kings 19:11–12

The Jesus Whisperer introduces a supernatural impartation, a transformation from the world's view to God's voice—the difference between darkness and light. This method is one step beyond a natural method of hearing to a deeper sensitivity "as deep calls unto deep."

Jesus instructed me to write this book, and He even gave me the title, which I believe defines its purpose. His purpose is love, and to be a *Jesus Whisperer* is to lead by love. The purpose of the book goes beyond my personal agenda, as I believe it was written as a trusted, biblical scribe of old would write inspirations. These scribes had revelation when the Holy Spirit came upon them, and they were given the divine unction to communicate them on a scroll as a record. The difference between then and now is that since the Day of Pentecost, we are temples of the Holy Spirit: "Your body is the temple of the Holy Spirit who is in you, whom you have from God" (1 Corinthians. 6:19). Indeed, He no longer comes upon us, but He rises from within as we discern His voice. That same gift, thought to be the anointing of the Holy Spirit, is of the utmost importance for such a time as this.

The Jesus Whisperer speaks of a personal relationship with God. He desires to have this communion with all His children, and He has given us the Holy Spirit for instruction. As we learn to incline our ear to Him, He compels us to pursue the more excellent way of love, helping us to discern His still and gentle voice and to walk the path He has set before us. If we know and follow His voice, we will be equipped for a victorious life.

Heavenly Father

I am written in Your Books, more than one I am told
You have whispered secretes in my heart and
given treasures more than gold

You gave me time and freedom so much more than I deserved
So many choices within my reach and the riches of Your Word

You never forced upon me Your presence or Your way
You waited for a willing heart teaching me to pray

Yet the moment I returned repentant and undone
You ran to me with me Signet Ring and Royal Robe
embracing me as one

Your gentle whispers from your heart flood my hungry soul
With the Gospel of good news for those desiring to be whole

Thank You for the privilege and the gift that gave me life
When Jesus whispered in my ear, "I want you as my wife."

Now I shout it from the mountain tops across the land and seas
You too can be a whisperer if you get down on your knees

Just trust the loving Lamb of God who took away your sins
Repent, surrender **all** my friend, and you will be ***born again***

Allow the Holy Spirit to fill you with His best
Then go and make disciples, God will do the rest

by Faun Collett

God instructed me to write this book to tell about my "first love." I offer it as a testimony of what He has done in and through my life and to teach others to follow His leading. I encourage you to pay close attention as you read through the pages of my life and learn to discern His voice for yourself. Though my trials and heartaches were overwhelming, flashes of memories would remind me that Jesus, the Whispering Hope of the Ages, has never left my side. Suddenly I could see because of His whispers. Hearing and learning to discern God's voice amidst the clamor of distractions and background noises requires spending time with Him. The anointing increases and our listening skills improve as we read the Bible and incline our ears to Him as we acquire the mind of Christ.

God gave me the title of this book when I attended a Treasure Coast Word Weavers Writers' Conference. As I put my hand on the door handle to enter the classroom, I clearly heard God speak: "The title of you book is *The Jesus Whisperer.*" With absolute clarity, I heard His words and embraced this title. What an honor it is to *whisper Jesus* to a lost and dying world. *First comes the whisper, then comes the shout!*

Man's Relationship with His Creator

In the holy Bible, the book of Genesis records the story of God's creation. Throughout biblical history, there have been scores of records in which men have claimed a divine connection with the Creator. When Adam and Eve lived in the Garden of Eden, their relationship with God and each other was undefiled until a suggestion was made by the enemy of their souls. The serpent was more sly and cunning than any beast of the field. This leads me to believe there were other sly and cunning beasts of the field—and they all could talk. In his deceitful, cunning way, the serpent asked Eve, "Did God *really* say you shall not eat of every tree of the garden?" With that question, one opportunity was presented...an opportunity to question God's voice and to critique His providence. From that time until now, this very question has tirelessly been repeated: Did God *really* say? It stands to reason that dialogue with a sly, cunning enemy can ruin a very good relationship, like the one Adam and Eve had with God.

There is no creature hidden from His light; all things are naked and open to the eyes of Him who is without sin. He sympathizes with our weaknesses, and in all points, He empowers us to hold fast to our confession and has enabled us by His love and sacrifice. *He passed through the heavens.* Jesus, the Son of God, empowers us to hold fast to our confessions, and He has enabled us by His love and sacrifice to come boldly to the throne of grace to obtain mercy and find help in time of need. He is the living Word, He is Powerful, and knowing His voice confirms His Word—you shall know the truth, and Jesus and the truth will set you free. Hearing His voice comes from spending time with Him in His Word so that these other voices become strange and you avoid them.

In the book of Genesis, the history of creation reveals that "In the beginning God created the heavens and the earth. The earth was without form, and void; and darkness was on the face of the deep. And the Spirit of God was hovering over the face of the waters" (Genesis 1:1). It is my belief that, just like in the beginning, God hovers over us and protects us, but He also grieves for us when we hurt. He longs for an intimate relationship with us, but first we must listen for His *whispers*—and then we must just breathe.

Just Breathe

Breathe out, breathe in, breathe out, and breathe in,
For My Breath is your Breath,
so breathe life over your dominion,
Over your world, over your realm of influence.
Breathe out My love, exhale My breath over the dead things,

Over the cursed things, and know this:
My breath is life and gives life.
My breath carries conviction and healing.
Your breath carries the living Word, and

The power of life and death is in your tongue.
When your breath is in My plans and purposes,
Your tongue will no longer be unruly.
Your tongue will be the muscle, the power to move

Here and there, in and out, to rule and reign,
to proclaim, to shout,
To call those things that seem are not,
until it is, and you cast out doubt,
Then you declare, decree, proclaim the former
and the latter rain.
You watch My breath, My tangible breath,
manifest My very best,
And all who hear, receive are blessed,
and will enter into My Sabbath rest.

by Faun Collett

God's Gifts Can Come in a Vision

God has placed giftings in all of us. As you journey with me, I want to share with you how He communicates through His gifting. *For example,* I once had a vision. In this vision, I saw a camel with its head raised toward the heavens, mouth open wide and a band around its head that covered its eyes. Glistening jewels were on its headband, reflecting the light of the sun. A spectrum of color bounced off the jewels. Every facet was catching sunbeams and projecting glory, emulating the *crowns* God has fashioned for us, His Bride.

As a beast of burden, the camel was stretching, tasting the air, and testing the atmosphere to assess in the desert places a path to the oases. By the relentless heat of day or by the cold of night, it found its way, by the compass of heaven within. It was prompted to seek out its Master and fulfill its destiny. Occasionally those it helped would unload their burdens so it could pass through the eye of the needle (a literal gate in the Middle East), the narrow way. I had the impression God was speaking to me about His giftings, and I heard His whisper, *"Likewise, will I not make a way for you where there seems to be no way? I have given you gifts to negotiate the Way. I have given you My Son, who IS the Way, and I have sent My Spirit to show you the Way."* I saw the camel as a voice—our voice—gifted and equipped.

Learning to Listen on Your Journey

During this time, God gave me a poem. It surpassed my own understanding about His love and His ultimate sacrifice. Retiring to my bedroom, a phrase began to flood my thoughts: "Shady side of Calvary's mountain" wooed me to sleep. The next morning, the phrase returned. I realized, *There were two sides to that mountain: a shady side and a sunny side.* I quickly grabbed a pen and piece of paper. With remarkable anointing, I began to write as He whispered to me. This incredible revelation was written quickly. In awe of His presence, I instantly recited the masterpiece, and He titled the poem "Two Sides to a Mountain."

Two Sides to a Mountain

Shady side of Calvary's mountain,
On a sad and dreary day,
Stood a crowd of angry people
In a dismal kind of way.

Their lives had been disrupted
By a man who said He's God,
And they didn't want His Kingdom
On their sacred chosen sod.

They had their own religion,
Certain rituals in their cult,
And they wouldn't let that Peasant say
He knew the end result.

So, they mocked Him, and they scorned Him,
Placed their stripes upon His back;
Threw a scarlet robe around Him.
In His precious face, they spat.

Then they made a crown of sorrow,
Piercing thorns upon a vine,
Pushed it deep into His temple,
Then they screamed, "Now He's divine."

"Hail, King of the Jews!" they shouted.
All His teachings they had scorned,
And He stood there as they mocked Him,
While for them, their souls, He mourned.

He was such a faithful servant,
While tribulation on Him laid.
He would have wished deliverance,
But His Father's will be obeyed.

So, He straightened up His shoulders,
Prayed for guidance from above,
Then He took the cross upon Him,
And He headed forth in love.

He suffered all that man could suffer
In His few years of thirty-three,
All the pain and grief and sorrow,
All of mankind's misery.

Yet He lived His life so perfect,
Man could never match His call,
And God so loved, He gave His gift,
His perfect Son, to all.

The worst was yet to happen,
The greatest burden was to be
Jesus Christ, our sinless Savior,
Took our sins upon that tree.

All our sins, past, present, future,
On His shoulders, they did rest,
And at that time, He was forsaken;
He withstood His final test.

Then He cried to God the Father,
"Why hast Thou forsaken Me?"
God must have said, "Son, don't You know,
"That sin, I cannot see."

For God, so pure, so holy,
Could not look upon that sin,
And Jesus made that final sacrifice
So a new life could begin.

A new life deep inside us,
All our sins were put away,
When we take the gift God gave, in faith,
For He the price did pay.

And in that final hour,
The crowd was awed as Jesus said,
"Father, I commend My Spirit,
"It is finished." *He was dead.*

But there was a sunny side to Calvary's mountain
That spread throughout the land,
For Christ our Lord was risen,
And that day was mighty grand.

He stayed to share His victory,
And His final witness gave:
"Go spread the word through all the world
"That Christ alone can save."

Then in all His splendid glory,
Outstretched arms to God above,
He ascended into heaven
To unite with God in love.

Here on earth, some men are searching,
But there are other men
Who await His final promise.
Jesus Christ will come again.

by Faun Collett

The Lord said, "Go out and stand on the mountain in the presence of the LORD, for the LORD is about to pass by" (1 Kings 19:11–13 NIV). God is clearly directing us to stay in His presence so we can cultivate a personal relationship with Him. If we lack the desire to be in His attendance, we will not hear His quiet *whispers* when He reaches out to us in times of need.

We all suffer the same kinds of sorrows, but we don't all make it to the mountaintops, and that is why it is so important to develop a true relationship with the Father, the Son, and the Holy Spirit. It takes a whisper from the Holy Spirit to bring us to that place where we can finally connect and eventually qualify to become a *Jesus whisperer.* From natural methods to training under the supernatural Spirit of the Living God, I discovered the truth. It is there where I was able to raise the dead, bring healing to the sick, and encourage the brokenhearted. *The Jesus Whisperer* will catapult anyone who hearkens to His voice into a power few have experienced. This power is what enables us to be delivered, set free, and thrive in His grace. *God's Word is truth and sharper than any two-edged sword, rightly dividing truth in our innermost parts, and that truth can set you free. There is a gift inside of you, placed there by your Maker, and that gift will make room for you.*

The Rhema word of God (the spoken utterance of God; individually, collectively, or specifically) will be a lamp unto your feet, a light to your path and a healing to all your bones:

Your word is a lamp to my feet and a light to my path.

—Psalm 119:105

Discerning God's Voice

Hearing and learning how to discern God's voice during myriad distractions and background noises is a skill developed as you incline your ear to Him. My father, sisters, and I learned a song at a little church in our neighborhood called "Hear Our Prayer, O Lord," and we sang it many times together a cappella: "Hear our prayer, O Lord. *Incline Thine ear to us* and grant us peace." The Father inclines His ear to us, and we need to incline our ears to Him. I was compelled to write this book by the Spirit of God, but I didn't have a title. After joining a Christian Writer's Guild, I signed up for a class during a convention. When I touched the handle of the door to enter the classroom, I clearly heard God speak to me. He told me the title of my book was to be *The Jesus Whisperer.* I didn't choose the title, nor would I have, but God spoke, and I don't question His word to me.

God's still, small voice became more distinctive than the loud voices of chaos and confusion bombarding my world. The Whispering Hope of the Ages carried me back to familiar flashes of memory as I recalled His presence in my life. Jesus had always been with me, softly calling, gently guiding, patiently waiting for me to cross over from the natural to a supernatural destiny by faith. My wilderness journey was over. I finally inclined my ear to Him, and I heard Him loud and clear. Jesus, the true Shepherd, said, "Most assuredly,

I say to you, he who does not enter the sheepfold by the door, but climbs up some other way, the same is a thief and a robber. But he who enters by the door is the shepherd of the sheep. To him the doorkeeper opens, and the sheep hear his voice; and he calls his own sheep by name and leads them out. And when he brings out his own sheep, he goes before them; and the sheep follow him, for they know his voice. Yet they will by no means follow a stranger, but will flee from him, for they do not know the voice of strangers" (John 10:1–5). Above all, I encourage you to get to know our heavenly Father. His desire is for you to follow Him: "There-fore, if anyone is in Christ, he is a new creation; old things have passed away; behold, all things have become new" (2 Cor. 5:17). He gave us free will and the choice to come to Him out of love and acceptance.

As I think back to that time when I clearly heard *His voice* at the hospital where I worked, I realized He had spoken to me many times before, but the noise of distrac-tions blindsided me, and I became insensitive to that *still, small voice.* Even the prophet Elijah, stifled by fear at the proclamation Jezebel made to take his life, panicked and tried to hide from the enemy. Even in his time of weakness, when he wanted to give up and die, God sent an angel to awaken him, who said, "'Arise and eat....'" And there by his head was a cake baked on coals and a jar of water. So he ate and drank, and lay down again." That sounds like typical behavior of someone who is exhausted and depressed, doesn't it? But look at what happened next, as "the angel of the Lord came back the second time, and touched him, and said, 'Arise and eat, *because the journey is too great for you.*'" (1 Kings 19:5–7).

As I reflect on Elijah, I am reminded of how many times angels in disguise came during my darkest hours and offered me spiritual food, refreshing, encouraging, and strengthening me beyond measure. It was in these desolate places that I cried out to God and went from the deepest valley to a breathtaking mountaintop in a moment of time.

God works in mysterious ways—through friends, family, the Church, and even the stranger on a Jericho road. In Elijah's case, during the time when he was fleeing for his life, God gave him a revelation, and it speaks volumes to a lost and dying world. The word of the Lord came to Elijah on top of Horeb, the mountain of God. (Mount Horeb means "horrible mountain.") It is interesting to me that God shows up and gives us our breakthrough right at the horrible mountains in our life. In 1 Kings, God spoke directly to Elijah and said, "'Go out, and stand on the mountain before the Lord.' "And behold, the Lord passed by, and a great and strong wind tore into the mountains and broke the rocks in pieces before the Lord, but the Lord was not in the wind; and after the wind an earthquake, but the Lord was not in the earthquake; and after the earthquake a fire, but the Lord was not in the fire; and after the fire a still small voice. So it was, when Elijah heard it, that he wrapped his face in his mantle and went out and stood in the entrance of the cave. Suddenly, *a voice came to him, and said, 'What are you doing here, Elijah?'"* (1 Kings 19:13). This Scripture demonstrates that God had a relationship with Elijah because Elijah had inclined his ear to God and wanted to hear the deeper thoughts of His heart. God could speak to Elijah in the dark and hiding place of a mountain cave, just like God wants to connect with you when you hide in the darkest places of your earthly world, so you can hear His voice (His *whispers*) and be comforted wherever you are.

Building My Personal Relationship with God

Relationships take work and dedication; for me, my relationship with the Holy Spirit depends on my willingness to seek Him and listen to His voice as He *quietly whispers* to me. In response to a very clear ministry calling, I continued to study the Word of God to show myself approved. I was ordained under Pat Harrison, the daughter of Kenneth Hagin Sr. and the wife of Buddy Harrison, publisher/founder of Harrison House Publishing. It's interesting to note that almost all of those called to that ministry had an anointing to prophesy in rhyme, as did I. When we would attend assemblies, it was very common to give and receive a word under that kind of anointing. I was licensed in 2002 and ordained in 2004, and I continued under Pastor Terry and Becky Roberts at FCFC, Warrenton, Missouri. They served the church in two separate locations, the Wentzville and Warrenton campuses, with close to two thousand members. I am still licensed under them to officiate any weddings or funerals in the state of Missouri.

During that time, I also ministered to many different denominations as Rainbow the Musical Clown, bringing the Gospel to the Catholic Church School, teaching and preaching at Methodist churches, Presbyterian churches, and some churches in other states. In 1995, Doug and I began the Academy of Missouri Educational Network of Graduate Dogs, Inc., and I worked a foster program and an at-risk program as well as a step down and recovery program later down the road. This is what I have done in preparation to answering my call. If I had to define a call from God in any given area, I would say I am equipped to teach, instruct, counsel, and impart what has been imparted to me in the Body of Christ for over fifty years. I have a prophetic gift, and I have operated in that anointing. The last time Pastor Harold came, he spoke over me and said I had a calling in the area of prayer. That is a calling I want to honor to the best of my ability. I believe we all have that call, and as we develop our relationship with the unction of the Holy Spirit, we will see much more of a demonstration of *His power*, with signs and wonders released in this community.

> He who sins is of the devil, for the devil has sinned from the beginning. For this purpose, the Son of God was manifested, that He might destroy the works of the devil.
>
> —1 John 3:8 NKJV

The Holy Comforter

Most of us don't know what lies ahead or when we will die, and for that reason, we should have an inner urgency to listen to the Holy Spirit and build a relationship with Him that will comfort us during times of personal trials and struggles. We live in a sinful world. Bad things happen! But it was not supposed to be this way, and more importantly, it will not always be this way! God has a plan, and it goes beyond what we now know.

God has made a way for sinful people (including you and me) to be with Him in a perfect world! *The way is Jesus!* If you've never asked Him to be your Savior, then acknowledge that you have sinned and that you have a serious problem before you, in light of a God who is perfect and just. *Recognize there is nothing you can do to save yourself, and trust Jesus, who died to pay the penalty for your sin.* He has risen from the dead and wants to make a trade with you!

He wants to take all of your unrighteousness and give you all of His righteousness. This is the way to know God and someday be free from this pain-ridden world.

We grieve when we lose a loved one, but each of us is dying, too! No one knows if they will even see tomorrow, but perhaps the suffering that is taking place in this world today is because God is waiting for you to acknowledge your sin and turn to Him for forgiveness; this grace must occur before you or I can start to build a relationship that holds the promise of eternal life. Perhaps you are the one whom Jesus is waiting for before He can return! Jesus suffered on the cross for you. God did not spare Him, but He told us to share in His sufferings! Why would He spare me if my suffering would result in good for you? If my sufferings are the means by which God can bring even one person to Himself, then it is an honor for me to have suffered, but you must understand that God is good and brings no evil upon us. He created us with free will, and He gives us the opportunity to choose our own destiny and the place where we will spend our eternal life.

It is important to remember that we are in a fight, a fight of faith, and we have been given the ultimate victory, but we must labor to enter God's rest. So, my words to you are these! Remember that *the Bible is the infallible Word of God* and that all things must be filtered through the Word of God!

And finally, this I shout from the heavens: Seek to know God and read the Word, serve with joy, and finish strong as you build your personal relationship with God! Don't just listen for the Holy Spirit's whispers but do the work; take heed to build your relationship with God based on a resilient faith, then walk out your destiny and take charge. You are more than a conqueror through Jesus Christ, who strengthens you. He made you to win! Be strong in the Lord and the power of His might! Connect to His Body, tend to His house, and serve!

> "I am the way, the truth, and the life. No one comes to the Father except through Me."
>
> —John 14:6 NIV

Steps to Know Him and Stay Strong in Faith

Step One—Get to know Him.

Step Two—Allow the Holy Spirit to have His way.

Step Three—Listen as He calls, and He will bring you out of darkness into His glorious light.

Step Four—Be equipped and empowered by the Holy Spirit.

Step Five—Be filled with His Spirit and the kind of anointing that breaks every chain.

Step Six—Honor His memory and spend time in His presence.

Prayer

Our Father in heaven, may we always show the utmost respect for Your holy name. Jesus taught us to pray that way. Every name describing You in the Holy Bible deserves honor. You are our sanctification, and You set us apart for special treatment. Your name is like an ointment of salvation, healing, peace, provision, and divine protection. You are our Shepherd, and Your banner over us is love. Hallowed be Thy name! There is none like You, and You alone deserve the glory. May we enter Your gates by the blood of the Lamb of God, who takes away the sins of the world and worship You with thanksgiving in our hearts. You are a good, good Father! Amen.

Notes

Chapter 3

The Written Word of God

The New Testament tells us that "love is patient, love is kind. It does not envy, it does not boast, it is not proud. It does not dishonor others, it is not self-seeking, it is not easily angered, it keeps no record of wrongs. Love does not delight in evil but rejoices with the truth" (1 Corinthians 13:4–6 NIV).

As I reflect on the passage above, I am reminded of my imperfections and how much I need His *love* to light my path through life. I am not perfect now, nor was I ever. That is why I must stay steadfast as His servant and guard my faith in the heavenly Father, His Son, and the Holy Spirit.

God Teaches Us Love and the Importance of Forgiveness

The Bible says, "Hope deferred makes the heart sick, but a longing fulfilled is a tree of life" (Proverbs 13:12 NIV).

Some translations say, "But desire fulfilled is the wellspring of life." What triumph! The wellspring of life! A tree of life! Isn't that what was in the Garden, and isn't that what God protected from man until man could be restored to eternal life so that his heart, mind, spirit, and intentions were pure and so that sin (darkness) had no place? Jesus prayed to the Father for us, for unity.

This defines love, declaring that without it, we are nothing but a loud, clanging cymbal or a noisy gong. It states that if we have faith to move mountains, but we have not love, we are nothing. If we give all we possess to the poor and surrender our bodies to the flames, but we don't have love, we gain nothing. Sometimes we think we have love, but our concept or understanding of love may be different from the kind of love God is talking about.

Many years ago, I faced unspeakable rejection from a man I married when I was young, and eventually there was divorce. God hates divorce, and so do I, but when someone leaves, you need to let it go. As his wife, I had been faithful. I had declared to God that I loved him so much, but he didn't love me in return. I made a list of all the hurtful, painful things he had done to me, and then I recorded all the good things I had done to win his love and affection to no avail. I told God that I loved my husband, but he didn't love me. God's response to me was not to come in agreement with my declaration about how hurtful my husband was.

Instead, He simply *whispered*, "So you think you love him? Let's take a look at real love." Of course, when I opened my Bible to 1 Corinthians 13:4–6, I began to see that my definition of love and God's definition of love were very different. As a matter of fact, everything that love was, I wasn't. I was not very patient, not too kind, very envious, somewhat rude because of the way I was being treated, a little self-seeking, easily angered, and I had a record of his wrongs a mile long. I was jealous, couldn't trust, lost hope, and did not persevere. With a repentant heart, I grabbed a piece of paper and penned my revelation. I titled the poem "The Battleground."0

The Battleground

Dear Lord, in Jesus' name I pray,
Please wash my guilt and sins away
Give me the strength to shun the wrong
And praise Thy name with loving song.

My body's like a battleground,
Myself a hindering force,
But deep inside this fortress,
My faith must chart its course.

And like all war-worn battlegrounds,
Though victory sings her song,
My soul has been so trampled down,
And it somehow seems so wrong.

And I'm weary of this battle, Lord,
That wages war within.
And I beg of Thee protection
From my enemy of sin.

And, Lord, though I'm not worthy
By Thy grace I'm glory-bound.
I just pray a special prayer of peace
For this old battleground.

Inspired by God's Word,
Faun Collett

It is important for you and me to know that we never have to face our battles alone. We were not intended to battle this world unaccompanied; our hearts desire reassurance, and God is the only One who can fill that empty spot of longing with hope, peace, and comfort.

Can We Hold Bitterness and Still Love?

To love like Jesus loves! Jesus prayed for us to have unity. What does that mean, and how is that possible? Jesus demonstrated what a true servant is! He laid down His deity and took the lowest of positions to identify with us and minister to us. He washed His disciples' feet as an example of humility, and He covered humanity with His blood. If we want to be like Him, we must serve like He served. *That's love in action.*

This is what Jesus taught. He said in the book of Luke, "Suppose one of you has a servant plowing or looking after the sheep. Will he say to the servant when he comes in from the field, 'Come along now and sit down to eat'? Won't he rather say, 'Prepare my supper, get yourself ready and wait on me while I eat and drink; after that you may eat and drink'? Will he thank the servant because he did what he was told to do? So you also, when you have done everything you were told to do, should say, 'We are unworthy servants; we have only done our duty'" (Luke 17:7–10 NIV). We must remember that we are not worthy, but because of Jesus' sacrifice, we are redeemed from our sins, and our salvation is bought by the blood of Jesus Christ.

The Parable of the Unmerciful Servant

The Parable of the Unmerciful Servant is found in *Matthew 18:21–35* and expounds on debt that the servant could never repay, as he demanded a far lesser debt from his fellow servant and without mercy having him thrown into debtors' prison with his entire family until the debt was satisfied. The other servants were greatly distressed and went to their master and told him everything that had happened. "The master called [in the unmerciful servant]. 'You wicked servant,' he said, 'I canceled all that debt of yours because you begged me to. Shouldn't you have had mercy on your fellow servant just as I had on you?' In anger, his master handed him over to the jailers [some translations say "tormentors"] to be tortured until he should pay back all he owed" (NIV). Remember, it was a debt he could never repay.

Jesus gives us clear directions on love and forgiveness. After all, God sent His only Son, Jesus, to die on the cross so our sins could be forgiven. How important is this to God? Let us look in the book of Matthew to focus on the importance of reconciliation: "Therefore, if you are offering your gift at the altar and there remember that your brother or sister has something against you, leave your gift there in front of the altar. First go and be reconciled to them; then come and offer your gift" (Matthew 5:23–24 NIV).

Hebrews 12:14–15 says: "Pursue peace with all people, and holiness, without which no one will see the Lord: looking carefully lest anyone fall short of the grace of God, lest any root of bitterness springing up cause trouble, and by this many become defiled."

God Instructs Us to Live in Peace

"If it is possible, as far as it depends on you, live at peace with everyone. Do not take revenge, my dear friends, but leave room for God's wrath, for it is written: 'If it is possible, as much as depends on you, live peaceably with all men. Beloved, do not avenge yourselves, but rather give place to wrath; for it is written, "Vengeance is Mine, I will repay," says the Lord.'"

—Romans 12:18–19

God wants us to have peace and focus on Him instead of the wrongs we have experienced. If we focus on the wrongs that others have done to us, we let bitterness and hate creep into our hearts, and we risk our eternal relationship with our heavenly Father. It is important to remember that our bond with the Father should be more important to us than any separation from man.

In one of my sermons, I used a visual example with a little clip from the movie *The Lion King*. It was about a lioness that was bitter, resentful, and *unforgiving*. The entire pride of lions wanted to embrace and include her, but she couldn't let go of her bitterness and so she perished. There are some who will fight to the death and refuse the hand of friendship or the loving embrace of fellowship. God's Word tells us to forgive and we will be forgiven, or we place ourselves under judgment and perish. The Scriptures says that as much as it is possible with you, be at peace and offer peace. God has given us the ministry of reconciliation.

God has done all this. He has restored our *relationship* with Him through Christ and has given us this ministry of restoring relationships. So many, many times we look at sickness and death as an outward assault from the enemy. Yet it is highly possible that we are our own worst enemies, refusing to embrace the better way of love and unwilling to let go of bitterness, resentment, and sometimes even hatred because somebody done somebody wrong. Wake up, Church! Stop coming into agreement with the father of lies. *Satan is always* the accuser of the brethren. Remember, love covers a multitude of sins. When Jesus taught us the Lord's Prayer, He said, "Forgive us our trespasses as we forgive those who trespass against us and lead us not into temptation but deliver us from evil."

When we seek peace and surrender to love instead of hate, we acquire freedom. He whom the Son sets free is free, indeed. The chains are broken and no longer hold us in bondage. At this place we set things right, and our own hearts will no longer condemn us. We can come boldly into the throne room and pray with confidence. Here we can declare and decree, rule and reign, with authority. Along with faith, hope, and love, we can embrace the victory that Jesus purchased for His Bride! Let us prefer one another in love and be healed.

As you read the following poem, which God quietly *whispered* to me, I personally encourage you to immerse yourself in God's Word, the Bible, so you can strengthen your relationship with Him and not miss your mark in heaven's rewards. The following poem was given to me as a prophetic message during a service at Faith Christian Family Church, while Reverend Pat Harrison ministered the Word of God.

Missing the Mark

So, what have I said, how do you begin?
Discover how I have identified SIN.
It's missing the mark—it's what you have missed
When I've come to help, and you resist.

When I've come to lead and seek to IMPART
But find a hard, unyielding heart,
Missing the mark when I've called you out,
But you don't understand and begin to pout.

It's what you've missed when I come to teach,
But you've made up your mind and stand just out of reach,
When you have decided to religiously stay,
Embracing the natural, going your way.

You've been missing the mark, missing out on My plan,
Secure in the sensible schemes of man,
But you'll never be satisfied, you'll never be filled
Unless you have trusted My PURPOSEFUL WILL.

So, SIN is NOT just what you've done to Me.
It's what you've MISSED OUT ON
When you could have been set free!

Inspired by the love of God,
Faun Collett

Each one of us has missed the mark in life, but God is patient, and the Holy Spirit is excellent at teaching us how to press in and develop our skills. When we miss the mark, remember what quenches the fiery darts of the evil one. As we get spiritually dressed every day with the whole armor of God, we must take the shield of faith and practice our skills with the sword of the Spirit (which is the Word of God), along with the skills of an archer who knows his target and uses his gifting to bring in the victory (even our faith, by the blood of the Lamb) that overcomes the world! PRACTICE TRUTH! You shall KNOW the truth, and the truth will set you free, indeed.

Unity in the Body

In Chapter 2, I emphasized the importance of knowing God's Word. If you want to hear His voice, one of the first steps you must take is recognizing His living Word. The next step is equally important. I began this book with a prayer to the Father, the Son, and the Holy Spirit. All three are embodied as one God, but They are unique in Their ministry, and They complement each other. Even so, it is difficult to some fainwho have never been taught about God in three persons. If your connection to God is hindered because you do not know His Holy Spirit, it will cripple you from hearing His voice. You cannot hear from the Holy Spirit unless you know

Him. He is the exact representation of Jesus, and He is here now to instruct, equip, and empower us to be overcomers.

In the book of John, Jesus said, "And the glory which You gave Me I have given them, that they may be one just as We are one: I in them, and You in Me; that they may be made perfect in one, and that the world may know that You have sent Me, and have loved them as You have loved Me" (John 17:22–23). It is important to focus on God's plan and understand that you see the Father, Son, and the Holy Spirit are in unity and that He wants you to be in unity with Him. In the book of Ephesians, God tells us to *live in unity:*

> I, therefore, the prisoner for the Lord, urge you to live worthily of the calling with which you have been called, with all humility and gentleness, with patience, putting up with one another in love, making every effort to keep the unity of the Spirit in the bond of peace. There is one body and one Spirit, just as you too were called to the one hope of your calling.
>
> —Ephesians 4:1–4 NET

God wants us to be at peace and trust in Him, His Son, and the Holy Spirit. My spiritual goal is to trust in Him and to listen for His quiet *whispers*, which will guide me in my service for God.

Not long ago I was invited to be a guest speaker at New Hope Church. After much prayer, a message was placed on my heart, and I delivered a sermon on *"Unity in the Body of Christ."* If our hearts condemn us, God is greater than our hearts, and He knows all things. Beloved, if our hearts do not condemn us, we have confidence toward God. And whatever we ask, we receive from Him, because we keep His commandments and do those things that are pleasing in His sight. And this is His commandment: that we should believe on the name of His Son, Jesus Christ, and love one another, as He gave us commandment to do.

> And now these three remain: faith, hope and love. But the greatest of these is love.
>
> —1 Corinthians 13:13 NIV

> Hope deferred makes the heart sick, but a longing fulfilled is a tree of life.
>
> —Proverbs 13:12 NIV

It is important to remember that Jesus and His sacrifices have given us hope that was not manifested to us before the first coming of Jesus Christ. It is there that the Lord bestows His blessing, even life forevermore. This is the ultimate goal of eternity: love! Love covers a multitude of transgressions. It's the greatest commandment: "'You shall love the Lord your God with all your heart, with all your soul, and with all your mind.' This is the first and great commandment. And the second is like it: 'You shall love your neighbor as yourself" (Matthew 22:37–39). Jesus knew a house divided against itself could not stand. We should immerse ourselves in the Scriptures and know the Word so we do not fall away from Him.

> How good and pleasant it is when God's people live together in unity!
>
> —Psalm 133:1 NIV

> It is as if the dew of Hermon were falling on Mount Zion. For there the Lord bestows his blessing, even life forevermore.
>
> —Psalm 133:3 NIV

A Ministry of Reconciliation

Scripture says that as much as is possible with you, you should be at peace and offer peace. God has given us the ministry of reconciliation. First Corinthians 5:18 says: "Now all things are of God, who has reconciled us to Himself through Jesus Christ, and has given us the ministry of reconciliation."

After my divorce, I was wounded, but I sought God's grace and forgiveness so I could let go of the anger and disappointment that was keeping me at arm's length from God. God clearly made me aware that I would only stand before Him accountable for how I lived my life. I needed to let Him take care of my husband and concentrate on offering myself up as a living sacrifice to the Lord, which was acceptable and good to Him. As it says in The New Testament: "And whenever you stand praying, if you have anything against anyone, forgive him, that your Father in heaven may also forgive you your trespasses" (Mark 11:25). That's where many of us miss the mark: holding someone's sin against them, instead of letting go and letting God. It's funny because before God talks about unity in the Body, He talks about unity between a husband and wife. The two shall become one.

It is important to ask yourself if you are coming to God's table with resentment toward your spouse, or even your family members, your friends, your brothers and sisters in Christ, your boss, your coworkers, or any of those in authority over you. Do you need to ask God for forgiveness? In the New Testament, we are given a powerful instruction on how powerful forgiveness is: "Judge not, and you shall not be judged. Condemn not, and you shall not be condemned. Forgive, and you will be forgiven" (Luke 6:37). How much are you willing to surrender or forgive to possess the kind of love that God wants you to have? I encourage you to steadfastly pray and reflect on the condition of your own heart when it comes to judging others or forgiving the people who hurt you.

In the spiritual realm, we can experience a strained relationship with God, which results from sinful behavior, and our own hearts will condemn us. The Scriptures tell us: "For if our heart condemns us, God is greater than our heart, and knows all things." And this: "Beloved, if our heart does not condemn us, we have confidence toward God" (1 John 3:20–21). In such a case, God desires to have our relationships restored. Such restoration of our relationship with God is because Jesus died for us on the cross, and if we accept Him, we are reconciled to God the Father. Paul also teaches us that "whoever eats this bread or drinks this cup of the Lord in an unworthy manner will be guilty of the body and blood of the Lord. But let a man examine himself, and so let him eat of the bread and drink of the cup. For he who eats and drinks in an unworthy manner eats and drinks judgment to himself, not discerning the Lord's body. For this reason many are weak and sick among you, and many sleep. For if we would judge ourselves, we would not be judged" (1 Corinthians 11:27–31). There is more to this than meets the eye. If we dig a little deeper and conduct a word study of these Scriptures, I'm sure we would discover even more about recognizing the Lord's Body, but suffice it to say that we need to carefully examine our hearts toward each other and love as Jesus loves.

Now all things are of God, who has reconciled us to Himself through Jesus Christ, and has given us the ministry of reconciliation.

—2 Corinthians 5:18

Prayer

Heavenly Father, Your Word is such a blessing to cherish and behold. The comfort in proclaiming Your power is pure gold. The clarity and knowledge, with the gift of understanding, provides a special kind of peace afforded to mankind! The peace, compounded interest, along with faith by measure, encompasses me with such an awesome earthy treasure. So many gifts, my King of kings, You alone have fashioned to illustrate the joy of being one and to demonstrate Your passion. You are such a limitless Giver, lavishing pure love, opening windows of heaven, endowing from above. What can I do to honor You? How can I bless You, Lord? What can I give to You, my King, but a yielding and grateful heart with abundant thanksgiving? Amen.

Notes

Chapter 4

The Holy Spirit—His Purpose—He Is God

Jesus tells us that "the Helper, the Holy Spirit, whom the Father will send in My name, He will teach you all things, and bring to your remembrance all things that I said to you" (John 14:26). The Holy Spirit is here now to instruct us and empower us as an exact representation of Jesus to fulfill the Gospel.

When I was first exposed to the teachings of the Holy Spirit, it was totally foreign to me; and nothing about it seemed like God. My preconceived ideas of the Holy Spirit were very unsettling and negative. I thought the Spirit was all about emotionalism, and as I envisioned people running up and down the aisles of a church and rolling on the floor, I wanted no part of it.

When I was invited to a Pentecostal church by a young friend, I immediately felt that the congregation was working themselves up in order to connect with God. To me, the serene reverence I had experienced in the Congregational Church was violated, and I was extremely uncomfortable as I observed people babbling in unknown tongues and seemingly out of control. It was completely contrary to the atmosphere of worship that I was accustomed to, in which there was a hushed reverence so as not to disturb the presence of God.

It wasn't until many years later that I was willing to lay down my preconceived ideas of religion and seek God's desire for worship. In His presence, there is fullness of God. He wants His children to be happy, blessed, and whole. His ways are higher and better than ours. When I saw in the Bible how the children of Israel worshiped, I was enlightened. King David said, "I was glad, very glad when they said to me let us go to the house of the Lord today there will be singing, there will be dancing, there will be victory in the house of the Lord today." Because the Holy Spirit was rarely mentioned in the Church, and it was seemingly a controversial subject, His presence was seldom discussed, and the importance of having a relationship with Him was not taught in the church culture that I was familiar with in my early journey of faith.

Mankind tends to put God in a box called religion, but it never works. God wants a pure and undefiled relationship with us, and that means we need to leave what was preconceived behind and press on to knowing the real truth of how the heavenly Father set up worship and what pleases Him. It's the truth that sets us free. Hype does not give us clarity. Seek first His righteousness and enroll your heart in the Holy Spirit school. Healing comes when our hearts are responsive to the Holy Spirit, His leading, and knowing Him is a wellspring of life.

The Jesus Whisperer is about hearing. In Chapter 2, I wrote about Elijah and his experience on the mountain. God came to Elijah to give him a prophecy for His people, and His presence was apparent to Elijah. If the Lord wasn't in the wind that fiercely smashed the rocks, or the earthquake, or the fire, then who was? This brings home an important point to me. The god of this world brings chaos, distraction, and confusion, and he wants to bend our ear to the natural circumstances so that we do not hear the *whispers* of our heavenly Father; however, the God of peace speaks in a still, small voice, and we need to train our ears to hear the true God in the midst of the storms.

God's mercy is new every morning, and it is from everlasting to everlasting; He is the Holy Spirit, and in Him we find the answers to eternal life we so desperately seek. If you knew Him, you would never run from Him, but you would run to Him to experience His healing and loving embrace. The *Bible is God's Word* and the only *truth*, as well as the only thing that really makes sense. Knowing Him and loving Him helped me to know love and connect to others who were facing life defeated. I know that many cultures, including ours, have unknowingly put God in a box. Religion is man's attempt to reach God, but Jesus is God's attempt to reach man through a relationship. Jesus had much to say about legalistic, man-made views instead of being led by the Holy Spirit. In almost every church in America, you will find rules and regulations that may seem contrary to the Word of God. That's why it is essential to pray and seek God as to where you should attend church and then take everything you hear back to the Holy Spirit and confirm it with the Word of God.

Christianity means "Christ in one." Jesus is the only Way. You can call yourself a car, sleep in garage, and try to drink gasoline, but that doesn't make you a car. It *will* make you sick and even kill you. Many in this country believe they are Christians, but they are deceived. Jesus said, "I am the way, the truth, and the life. No one comes to the Father except through Me" (John 14:6). We must reach out to Jesus Christ, confess our sins, pray for His forgiveness, and humble ourselves by believing that He is the Son of God, the truth, and the light. The Bible says this: "Therefore whoever humbles himself as this little child is the greatest in the kingdom of heaven" (Matthew18:4). We must be born again and invite Him into our hearts before we can dwell with Him in heaven.

Through all the roles I have had in life, I have had one purpose, to be like *Jesus* and to serve with joy! What defines me is my relationship with *Jesus*, and that's where I find peace—because He is the Prince of peace! Life throws a lot of curves our way, but when we become intimately acquainted with *Jesus, who is the Way, the Truth, and the Life, we're in better hands than All State.* (Allstate is a well-known insurance company that uses that as their slogan.) We also must foster the presence of the Father, Son, and the Holy Spirit in our lives. The apostle Paul put it this way: "Forgetting those things that are behind I reach towards the prize!" You might say he stumbled on that prize, but the truth is, his pride and religious arrogance had caused him to alienate the prize and blinded him to the treasure of real life!

Many may ask, Who is the Holy Spirit? Is He God? In the Bible, the Holy Spirit is described as fully God, along with God the Father and God the Son. The Bible says, "The Spirit of God was present in the creation" (Genesis 1:2). And "The Holy Spirit moved the prophets of God with the words of God" (2 Peter 1:21). He is the exact representation of Jesus on this earth, but He seldom gets the honor or attention He deserves. He came to enlighten us about things we don't know and give us a clearer picture of Jesus. If we don't acknowledge Him, we will miss the power and understanding we need to be overcomers. We are shown a resounding example of how the Holy Spirit is God in Acts 5:3–4. There, we are introduced to a man named Ananias, who was a man of God. God used Ananias to reach Paul (Saul) because God had a purpose for Paul. In turn, God used Ananias to restore Paul's sight because God had a plan to use Paul to spread His Word to the Gentiles.

There was another Ananias and his wife, Sapphira, who deceived the people, but they were unaware that they had lied to the Holy Spirit. After Paul began to fulfill his purpose, which was to spread the Word of God and Jesus' message, Peter confronted Ananias. Ananias had lied, and Peter said, "He had not lied to men but to God." God became disappointed with Ananias, and the Lord struck him dead because of his deception. I want to encourage you to read the Bible and study the Holy Spirit as it is shown in the book of Acts.

Meet the Holy Spirit, Our Victory in Christ

He Helps Us. "In the same way the Spirit also helps our weakness; for we do not know how to pray as we should, but the Spirit Himself intercedes for us with groaning's too deep for words" (Romans 8:26 NASB1995).

He Guides Us. "But when He, the Spirit of truth, comes, He will guide you into all the truth; for He will not speak on His own initiative, but whatever He hears, He will speak; and He will disclose to you what is to come" (John 16:13 NASB1995).

He Teaches Us. "But the Helper, the Holy Spirit whom the Father will send in My name, He will teach you all things, and remind you of all that I said to you" (John 14:26 NASB1995).

He Speaks. "The one who has an ear, let him hear what the Spirit says to the churches" (Revelation 2:29 NASB1995).

He Reveals. "For to us God revealed them through the Spirit; for the Spirit searches all things, even the depths of God" (1 Corinthians 2:10 NASB1995).

He Testifies of Jesus. "When the Helper comes, whom I will send to you from the Father, namely, the Spirit of truth who comes from the Father, He will testify about Me" (John 15:26 nasb1995). "And He, when He comes, will convict the world regarding sin, and righteousness, and judgment" (John 16:8 NASB1995).

He Comforts Us. "So the church throughout Judea, Galilee, and Samaria enjoyed peace, as it was being built up; and as it continued in the fear of the Lord and in the comfort of the Holy Spirit, it kept increasing" (Acts 9:31 NASB1995).

He Calls Us. "While they were serving the Lord and fasting, the Holy Spirit said, 'Set Barnabas and Saul apart for Me for the work to which I have called them'" (Acts 13:2 NASB1995).

He Fills Us. "And when they had prayed, the place where they had gathered together was shaken, and they were all filled with the Holy Spirit and began to speak the word of God with boldness" (Acts 4:31 NASB1995).

He Strengthens Us. "I pray that out of his glorious riches he may strengthen you with power through his Spirit in your inner being" (Ephesians 3:16 NIV).

He Prays for Us. "Now in the same way the Spirit also helps our weakness; for we do not know what to pray for as we should, but the Spirit Himself intercedes for us with groanings too deep for words" (Romans 8:26 NASB1995).

He Lives in Us. "Do you not know that you are a temple of God and that the Spirit of God dwells in you?" (1 Corinthians 3:16 NASB1995).

He Produces Fruit. "But the fruit of the Spirit is love, joy, peace, patience, kindness, goodness, faithfulness, gentleness, self-control; against such things there is no law" (Galatians 5:22–23 NASB1995).

He Gives Gifts. "Now to each one the manifestation of the Spirit is given for the common good. To one there is given through the **Spirit** a message of wisdom, to another a message of knowledge by means of the same Spirit, to another faith by the same Spirit, to another gifts of healing by that one Spirit, to another miraculous powers, to another prophecy, to another distinguishing between spirits, to another speaking in different kinds of tongues, and to still another the interpretation of tongues" (Corinthians 12:7 NIV).

He Leads Us. "For those who are led by the Spirit of God are the children of God" (Romans 8:14 NIV).

He Empowers Us. The last thing Jesus says on earth is found in Acts1:8: "But you will receive power when the Holy Spirit comes on you; and you will be my witnesses in Jerusalem, and in all Judea and Samaria, and to the ends of the earth" (NIV).

The Holy Spirit's Assignment on Earth

God's people have been admonished. Those who have ears to hear, eyes to see, and a heart to understand will be held accountable. We are living in the end of the end times. They are perilous times, but we as the Body of Christ have been positioned in this age for *such a time as this.* Those whom God calls, He equips, and He doesn't make mistakes. You and I are here to be a light and to shine so that all those in our realm of influence will see the "light of Christ." To whom much is given, much is required. We have not been placed here powerless. Jesus is sitting next to the Father making constant intercession for us, and we are never alone.

You're Never Alone

I've wept and been moved with compassion.
I've suffered and struggled with destruction and death.
I've hurt to the point that exceeds what you know,
To the depth of the trials of each test.

All the schemes that the enemy sets to employ,
All the forces that loom on this earth,
There's nothing that happens, nothing at all,
That can overcome what I have birthed.

Listen to Me! Understand what I say.
I feel more than you ever can,
And whatever Gethsemane you have to endure,
Such is common to man.

But children, I've paved the way of escape,
And trust Me, this, too, will pass.
You're NEVER ALONE! Believe Me, I CARE.
My best was saved for the last.

Mysteries are never revealed to all.
Some will turn their own way,
But the Mystery of Ages was birthed in you
(Colossians 1:26–27),
And I'm with you whenever you pray.

Now nestle your head on My pillow of love,
My Spirit will comfort your pain.
Whatever you face, you won't face it alone!
Remember the REASON I CAME!

Inspired by the love of Jesus,
Faun Collett

Our precious Holy Spirit has been sent in this dispensation to build up, exhort, encourage, comfort, and empower His Body. This is the time to be filled with His plans and to be empowered to overcome. God wants us to work for Him and to be His voice here on the earth, and He empowers us to step into the gap so we can lead others to Him. Our heavenly Father had a purpose when He sent His Son, Jesus, to save us from sin, and He has a purpose for you and me. He will use even the smallest of us to move the hearts of His people and show what His love can do in times of adversity.

God whispers to us to motivate us to step into the light and demonstrate His love—just like He did with an innocent baby like Tony Doe.

Tony Doe

In July 1984, I had what I call an "epiphany moment." My husband brought home a newspaper after work and placed it on the kitchen counter. I'll never forget what I saw as I walked into the room. My eyes locked on the front-page headlines of the *St. Louis*

Post-Dispatch: "Newborn Baby Found in Bottom of Affton Storm Sewer."

I could not believe such an atrocity could happen, and not far from where I had grown up! There was a picture of three county police officers examining the sewer, where a paramedic descended eight feet into the damp, cold, unforgiving pit. He then lifted a trash bag, in which a newborn baby boy, still covered with his mother's blood, was screaming for his life. Hypothermia, pneumonia, and a fractured skull had almost overcome the child, but his cries were heard, and deliverance was accomplished. A miracle from God was birthed out of the darkest situation.

The story of Tony Doe reminded me of another child who was thrown into a pit and how God intervened. The biblical story of Joseph the dreamer flooded my mind. God had gifted this boy with a special connection with Him through dreams, and his brothers were jealous. They planned to kill him, but instead they threw him into a pit and waited until slave buyers passed by. Joseph was sold into slavery by his brothers, and he ultimately ended up in a stinky, dirty prison in Egypt. Regardless of these seemingly impossible circumstances, God never left Joseph, but He continued to anoint and empower him, not only to overcome his environment, but also to maintain his faith and excel in his abilities, gaining favor with God and man.

The story of Joseph is remarkable, and it shows how God had a plan for him that would be fulfilled in God's appointed time. Through Joseph's story, God revealed His plan to bring deliverance and salvation to Joseph's entire household. When he faced his brothers once again, he told them not to fear. What they had meant for evil, God had turned around for good. Joseph was positioned next to the highest authority, Pharaoh, with all the benefits that came with that position, and he ruled with Pharaoh over all the land. I believed in my heart that what God did for Joseph, he could do for little Tony Doe.

Immediately I laid my hands on the picture in the paper and prayed: "Father, I don't know what You are going to do about this unthinkable deed, but I'm asking You to be this baby's godmother. I want to hold him, sing to him, tell him that Jesus loves him, and dedicate him to You." I never said anything to anyone about my request to God; I just prayed and believed. A few days later, I got a phone call from my youngest sister, Kim. She called to tell me she and her husband had been chosen by the county's Family Services Division to take little Tony Doe home from the hospital and foster him until he was placed in a permanent home. They were to protect his identity from the public and were not supposed to tell anyone who the baby was, but she felt strongly that she needed to tell me, and she wanted me to be there when they brought him home. I was there to greet him at the door as he was welcomed into our family.

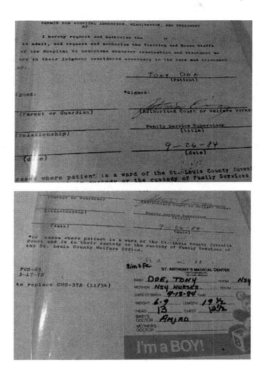

I gave little Tony Doe his first bath, sang "Jesus Loves Me" to him, and rocked him to sleep while I held him in my arms and prayed. It was a God thing, an epiphany moment, a divine encounter infused with love. The book of Jeremiah declares, "For I know the thoughts that I think toward you, says the Lord, thoughts of peace and not of evil, to give you a future and a hope" (Jeremiah 29:11). A few months later, I felt an urgency to take this precious gift whom God had placed with my baby sister and our family for a season and ask for prayer for him from the staff of Grace Church. Pastor Ron Tucker called the staff up to the front altar. With some beautiful worship music playing in the background, about fifteen people stood in a circle, and each one prayed a blessing over that precious baby, then passed him on to the next person. We anointed him with oil and then dedicated him to his Creator, knowing that what God begins, He perfects, and that little Tony Doe was in the palm of God's hand.

We were brokenhearted when Family Services came the very next day to take him away, but we were confident that if God was for him, nothing could stand against him. What was meant for evil, God would certainly turn around for good, and we felt very blessed to be a part of such a remarkable demonstration of love.

My sister Kim desperately wanted to adopt Tony, and she was devastated when that did not happen. When she was only twenty-four years old, she had been diagnosed with uterine cancer and was only given six months to live. I was in a fellowship called Day Spring at the time, and a young doctor who attended this group prayed with me for Kim. He also agreed to go to the hospital and pray for her with the laying on of hands. As he anointed her with oil and prayed, he felt as if God wanted him to talk to another young doctor who had just come to America from Greece. Another miracle was performed in our family's life when the young doctor said he wanted to try a radical surgery. He felt he could remove the cancer, even though our family had been told the tumor was inoperable. By the grace of God, Kim's surgery was successful.

Sadly, Kim would never be able to conceive and carry a child, but God had an even better plan. After Tony Doe was placed by Family Services with another family, Kim and her husband brought home a little four-year-old guy named Michael, who instantly captured our entire family with his affections. This miracle took place through a series of divine interventions. Michael's mom, Kathy, was rehabilitated. During that time, over Christmas, she visited one of our family gatherings. Little Michael was almost buried in gifts from all of us, and Kathy was overwhelmed with emotion. She had never witnessed such family love, peace, and joy. Jesus was our reason for celebration, and she not only received Him as her Lord, but she was welcomed into our hearts, as well. At the time, Kathy was pregnant, and she didn't want to abort the child; instead, she decided that Kim should adopt the baby.

Through almost impossible odds, God blessed Kim with the most delightful gift of all. She was with Kathy when the baby was delivered, and a healthy, bouncing baby boy named Dustin was placed in Kim's arms, and the adoption was official. Not only that, but when Kim went back to work, Kathy became Dustin's babysitter and never once claimed him as hers. She believed he was sent directly from heaven for Kim, and we believed it, too. Everyone was elated and praised God for His awesome plan, because little Dustin would grow into the most incredible blessing ever. Now Dustin has a beautiful bride, a new home, and two darling babies of his own.

The legacy of God's love goes on and on. His mercies are truly brand-new every morning, and they stretch from everlasting to everlasting as recorded in Lamentations: "Through the Lord's mercies we are not consumed, because His compassions fail not. They are new every morning; Great is Your faithfulness. 'The Lord is my portion,' says my soul, 'Therefore I hope in Him!' The Lord is good to those who wait for Him, to the soul who seeks Him. It is good that we would hope and wait quietly for the salvation of the LORD" (Lamentations 3:22–26). In the book of Psalms, we are given this assurance: "For the LORD is good; His mercy is everlasting, and His truth endures to all generations" (Psalm 100:5). We sought God's mercy with Tony Doe and with Kim during her struggles with cancer. We knew we served a merciful God, and He held us in the palm of His hands.

After Family Services took Tony Doe from our family, we did not know what happened to him, but we knew that God was in control. God had a purpose for Tony Doe, and that was evident from the time he was pulled from a dark and disastrous situation. He brought Kim from the depths of despair and rewarded her beyond measure. What a miracle-working God we have!

God's Purpose for Me and You

How comforting to realize that I am not alone and that whatever comes my way is no surprise to Jesus. He does no evil, but He gives me great comfort, power, and victory to overcome. Because I know that my battle is *not* against flesh and blood, I can see things in a new perspective, and I fight powers, principalities, and the rulers of darkness and wickedness in heavenly places. As I know who I am in Christ, put on the armor provided for me, take up the sword of God (the Word), and bind and loose with authority, my adversaries must flee from me.

We are to take captive every thought to make it obedient to Christ, and so we will be ready to punish every act of disobedience once our obedience is complete. Even now, as I approach the end of my earthly walk, I am learning to take authority as a believer more than ever before. I rule and reign in my realm of influence by walking in love, praying in the

Spirit, (1 Corinthians 12–14), and remaining focused on *glorifying God,* thus fulfilling my destiny in my generation. Being filled with the Holy Spirit has taken me to a whole new level in Christ, and it is a path I would never want to sidestep. Jesus is now sitting at the right hand of the Father. He said before He ascended that it was expedient for Him to go so the Holy Spirit could come. I would never want to be somewhere that the Holy Spirit is not welcome. He is the One here on earth now, and He came to give me *power.* The book of Acts says, "But you shall receive power when the Holy Spirit has come upon you; and you shall be witnesses to Me in Jerusalem, and in all Judea and Samaria, and to the end of the earth" (Acts 1:8). His power is what I need to complete the task the Father has set before me and fulfill His purpose for my life.

Passion Is Birthed by Purpose

This is the word given to me by the Holy Spirit: *Be on purpose, the appropriate time for the Lord. My time is measured by you. When you stand still, time stands still. When you move upon the earth by My Spirit, time is full—full of hope, full of purpose, full of faith, full of victory. Submit to Me, and let Me move through you so that your time is worthwhile, and My time is* **FULFILLED!**

The Lord whispered this to me as a prophetic word many years ago: *There are rocky places around the bend, rocky places in My river, but those river rocks are smooth from the washing of mighty water, and they cause a bubbling up, a bubbling up and refreshing splashes. They don't obstruct or retard My flow, but they cause My life to splash and spray and anoint My banks. Don't fear the rocky places. Welcome My mighty flow!*

"A Purpose to Lead and Feed" is a prophecy the Lord *whispered* to me during worship for the Body of Christ.

A Purpose to Lead and Feed

You weren't meant to save the world,
That's what Jesus came to do.
One crucifixion was enough
To lead the guilt-stained through.
But you were called to lead and feed
And sing the psalms of hope.
So many sheep have lost their sleep,
And they don't know how to cope.
I'm so glad for God's idea.
There is so much more to do.
The best idea He had for us
Is the one He had in you!

Inspired by the need to serve,
Faun Collett

So, I humbly ask, Has *God whispered* to you? What is your legacy? What will you leave behind for others? Your life is but a breath! Any breath of the flesh will evaporate in thin air, but *God's* life, *God's* breath, and *God's* Word will carry on into eternity. In this world, each breath of man is exchanged for oxygen, each moment energized with *purpose* to seize the day, but when you breathe in the *heavenly Father's* life and *His* plans and purposes, you will exchange a legacy of infinity. Because *God* lives, you will flourish forever, and you carry the breath of the *Holy Spirit!* As you exchange *Jesus'* life with others, *God* will energize His plans and *purposes* in the midst of death, in the presence of flesh. They will behold the blessings of your life in *God.* What a legacy! Someone once said, "Only what I've done for love's reward will stand the test of time!" When all is said and done, you are part of *God's* life when life is done! Real people, real *God*, real answers!

Prayer

Heavenly Father, Jesus taught us to pray, "Hallowed be Thy name," and that is a tall order on so many levels. Your name is multipurposed, and it exalts greatness in the incomparable measure of who You are. Although it has been recorded to show nearly one thousand names depicting the different personalities of God, indeed, one of my favorite Scriptures is found in Isaiah: "For unto us a child is born, unto us a Son is given, and the government shall be on His shoulders, and His name shall be called wonderful counselor, the mighty God, the everlasting Father, the prince of peace. Isaiah prophesied the Messiah's coming to save His people. Sweet Holy Spirit, You are the embodiment, the exact representation, of Jesus, and the One who is called our Helper, our Counselor, our Advocate, our Instructor. You came bearing gifts to equip us as believers. Even the least of Your gifts is more valuable than anything the world has to offer. Forgive us for not trusting You during this dispensation, and help us each to know You more and listen to Your quiet whispers for guidance and comfort. Amen.

Notes

Chapter 5

The Dispensation of Grace versus Lawlessness

All have sinned and fall short of the glory of God.

—Romans 3:23

Most of us do not know what lies ahead, including when or how we will die, but almost all of us resist being assaulted. When such events occur, many will blame God and will be angry that life is not fair!

Our sinful heart and nature says, "I don't believe this is the right thing for me, God!" Far too many think that God must not know what He is doing, or that if He does, He is not good, nor is He in control. Some believe He is just being unfair because He is not giving them what they want! That's what our sinful nature naturally says, and that's what your heart may say also! Our natural focus, which is typically self-importance, leads us to sin (miss the mark), and it's our greatest problem. Some may ask today why so many tragedies take place, but I don't ask why because I know the answer. Here it is.

We live in a sinful world! Bad things happen! But it was not supposed to be this way, and more importantly, it will not always this way! The world today is full of evil. Our schools are under attack from the demonic forces. Teachers are introducing philosophies into the curriculum that are detrimental to our youth. Morals, values, and ethics are being compromised for the sake of change, rather than for the glory of God. Change for what? It is definitely not for the benefit of our children. They are taught that tolerance of alternative lifestyles is acceptable and that it is the most important aspect of life. Teachers are not allowed to reference God, nor pray with our children, yet our children can be encouraged to think of the most ungodly things without reprisal. This grieves me for many reasons.

Our children spend more waking hours in school than they do with their parents. This alone is a frightening prospect for the spiritual well-being of our youth. Unfortunately, far too many parents do not attend church and are nonbelievers. This fact leaves our countries' youth at a disadvantage. Satan will attempt to enter their lives and take control. Lawlessness will worsen before Jesus returns to the earth, and it is one of the signs of the times.

Violence is prevalent in our schools, our streets, and our businesses. Murder, drugs, and alcohol are on the rise, and people are suffering from depression and a lack of hope. Families are in disarray, and mothers and fathers are not preparing their children with the moral values that will help guide them through the pitfalls of life. It is so urgent for us to teach our children that they do have godly choices in life. Our country is in moral decline, and abortion is rampant. Our precious Holy Spirit has been sent in this dispensation to build up, exhort, encourage, comfort, and empower us to overcome. You might ask, How do we do that? How can we overcome such adversities? We overcome by the blood of the Lamb! There is nothing He left out before He ascended. He did it all!

Recently I reflected on the condition of our world, and I sensed an urgency to finish this book because of the last-days demands on society. We are living in a time of what I would call warp-speed events. There have always been wars and rumors of wars, floods, earthquakes, and natural disasters, but these times are unparalleled. The world is in a turmoil more intense than at any other time in history. The information highway is congested with conflicting news and an overload of false data. A landslide of global media corruption with political controls is causing politics to quickly move toward a one-world order with an undisputable spirit-of-antichrist agenda. Weather changes with unforecastable disasters of compounded pollution buildup due to man's neglect coincide with new, uncontrolled viruses and deadly diseases lacing a panicked, fear-laden world. The following poem is a word I wrote in 2020, and it barely touches on all our present-day issues.

Suddenly

Suddenly the virus struck.
Without a hint it came.
Suddenly a quarantine,
Before I knew its name.

Suddenly fear manifest.
And media was deceiving.
Suddenly I found the faith
In what I'd been believing.

The leak came out of China,
From a region called Wu Han.
The WHO compelled to research
As the pandemic began.

Panic and pandemic
Formed allegiances worldwide,
And death stalked every nation
With no safe place to hide.

Life as most had known it
Hung precariously by a thread,
As mankind had no answers
And multitudes dropped dead.

Savage and contagious,
The consensus overall
Was to isolate the masses
With an impenetrable wall.

They shut down all the stadiums
The public gatherings,
Socials, schools, and libraries,
All sports events and teams.

Theaters, restaurants, day care,
The workplace and the mall,
Especially Christian seminars,
And churches most of all.

Except for the necessities,
Essential services evolved.
Walmart and the grocery stores,
The pharmacies were allowed.

Suddenly streets were empty.
State lines can't be crossed.
Families could not gather
When loved ones had been lost.

No family reunions or weddings,
No funerals could be planned.
There were no graduations, no prom,
No dances, and no band.

All around the world
Global lockdown was enforced.
Chaos, loss of jobs and income,
Domestic violence, suicide, hatred, and divorce.

Political upheavals,
Illuminati's want control.
Economies are falling.
New World Order is their goal.

The deep state showing disregard,
Socialistic tendencies are appalling.
Atheistic college agendas,
And blinded, you are falling.

Voter fraud is looming.
Gun laws are imposed.
Constitutional rights are threatened.
Child trafficking disclosed.

It happened, oh, so subtly,
While sickness filled the air.
A mystery unfolded,
Suddenly the world engaged in prayer.

While some began to panic,
Hoarding toilet paper and wipes,
Bibles started selling out
While airlines cancelled flights.

The "suddenly's" manifested
A peculiar kind of guise,
As suddenly believers
Were opening their eyes.

A call was rising in the soul
Of those who had been sleeping:
"If My people, called by My name
"Repented with their weeping…"

As strange as it seems,
It happened this way.
They humbled themselves
And began to pray.

They turned form their sins
And their wicked ways,
And God heard them from heaven,
Embracing their praise.

Then suddenly around the world,
While men were pursuing God's Word,
"I Am" began to heal the land.
His voice alone was heard.

by Faun Collett

The last stanza of this poem highlights the main purpose of this book: It is time that we hear His voice with clarity and confidence because God wants us to be empowered, protected, and sealed with His promise. Now is the time. No matter where you are, God is calling you to draw closer to Him than ever before. He is a good, good Father, and He has hope, a future, and a destiny for each of us if we will draw near to Him. The Bible says, "Or do you despise the riches of His goodness, forbearance, and longsuffering, not knowing that the goodness of God leads you to repentance?" (Romans 2:4). I encourage you to draw closer to our Lord Jesus Christ. Lean on Him for understanding and follow Him instead of the evil one that runs rampant in the world today.

God's Answer to Lawlessness

According to statistics, roughly 1.8 people die every second. In a world population that is currently close to seven billion people, roughly 33 percent of the world's population are believers, which means that close to 67 percent are not. By these figures, over four thousand people die every hour without Christ in their lives, every twenty-four hours of every day. Approximately one hundred thousand people are entering eternity each day, separated from God and sealed to a fate of eternal suffering and torment! That fact grieves me to the core of my being. We as Spirit-filled, born-again Christians are the vessels whom God has called to bring the light of Christ to a lost and dying world!

God has a plan, and it goes far beyond what you now know. He has made a way for sinful people (you and me) to be with Him in a perfect world! The way is Jesus! If you've never asked Him to be your Savior, then acknowledge that you have sinned and that you have a serious problem before you, in light of a God who is perfect and just. Recognize there is nothing you can do to save yourself, and *trust Jesus,* who died to pay the penalty for your sins. He has risen from the dead and wants to make a trade with you! He wants to take all your unrighteousness and give you all His righteousness. This is the way to know God and someday be free from this world and its pain.

When I pray the Lord's Prayer, the Regal Prayer, and I pray the words, "hallowed be Thy name," I am breathless. He is my sanctification, my salvation, my peace, my success, my Healer, my Provider, my Banner, my Shepherd, and so much more. Jesus became everything He hated, so that we could become everything He loves. He thought of it all, and He said it all. He told us to wait for the Holy Spirit. It was expedient that He go so that the Comforter could come and teach us all things about Him. The Comforter is here—He is here. And He has given us the power to overcome by the blood of the Lamb—and something else, the word of our testimony.

So, my words to you are these! Remember that the *Bible is the infallible Word of God* and that all things must be filtered through it! And finally, this I shout from the heavens: Know

God, read the Word, serve with joy, and finish strong! Don't just be a hearer, but do the Word, build your faith, walk out your destiny, and take charge.

God Gives Us the Opportunity to Choose

In God's *whispering voice,* He gave me the following prophecy: *In the early days, My people walked in discovery and opportunity to be connected to Me, to walk in truth and with truth. They had distractions due to angry, vengeful spiritual forces who sought residence to be empowered. Yes, distractions existed, but busyness was not one of them. Choices have always been set before My people, and My voice embodied the choice of life. Any other voice carried rebellion, separation, and spiritual forces that breed death. You say that was then, this is now! So, what about now, when a deluge of choices has choked free will? As the labor pains quicken and the birth is two centimeters away from the breakthrough, it is too late for a C-section. The choice must be made to press into delivery. I have cried by My Spirit: CHOOSE LIFE. Day by day, generation by generation, without regard to culture, color, or creed, I have broken through every dominion. BY MY SPIRIT, MY VOICE HAS RESOUNDED, TO CHOOSE LIFE. Those who have ears, let them hear. You are just two centimeters away— two centimeters away from a new heaven and a new earth, two centimeters away from your breakthrough. SO, WHAT ABOUT NOW? LISTEN TO ME!*

You Must Hear My Voice

Listen to Me, you must hear My voice
Before you can see.
You must put busyness far away,
Drawing nearer to Me in your busy day.

You must guard your heart
And protect your mind.
You must choose life
Or be left behind.

As a man knows a woman,
So must you know Me.
We must commune by My Spirit
With passionate intimacy.

Only then, only then, are the captives set free.
This is now, but what about then?
I have called you to be fishers of men,
If by making a choice you press into Me.

I will anoint your life,
Empower your BUSY,
And we will set the captives free
TOGETHER.

by Faun Collett

Remember that God has given you and me a choice, and you are *more than a conqueror* through Jesus Christ, who strengthens you; He made you to win! Be strong in the Lord and in the power of His might! Connect to His Body, tend to His house, and serve! A perfect example of this servitude is God's ability to work through you and me. We must commit to God and be willing to serve. We must listen for His soft whispers as He guides and directs us on our path of serving and working for Him with love and determination to spread His Word.

A perfect example of serving the Lord took place when one elderly lady heard the pastor's appeal one day to use the gifts God has given you and plug in to the Church. She wanted to serve, and she asked her pastor what she could do. The pastor asked her to talk to the assistant pastor. She had never prayed out loud before and said she never would, but the assistant pastor gave her a list of phone numbers and told her that when she had time, she could call people in the church to see if they had any prayer requests. She would then write them down and turn them in at the end of the week, so the staff could pray, but she began to pray for them as well.

Every night around 10 p.m., this little lady lifted people in prayer, and every week she called from her list members of the church to see if they had any special requests. Then one day she was at a restaurant, and a very old lady fell and broke her hip. When the paramedics came and put her on a stretcher to take her to the hospital, without hesitation she went over, took the lady's hand, and asked if she could pray for her. When it was all said and done, she marveled at the grace of God and realized that the deep things God had placed on the inside of her had manifested with a boldness she'd never had before, and she could not wait to tell me that she prayed out loud in front of those paramedics and the crowd of people standing around. The old lady was so thankful, and she felt so blessed that God had touched them both.

There is so much to do! Do something and do it as unto the Lord! The mystery of the ages is Christ in you, the hope of glory! Activate what is already inside you! **Push; press through** (Philippians 3:13–14). Finish strong!

A Ministry of Helping Others:

During my earthly life, my husband, Doug, and I went on a journey to help many who have faced broken homes and broken lives. I believe God placed a deep desire in both of us to help others, lead them to greener pastures and divert the lawlessness in their lives. We had the privilege to introduce them to the "Good Shepherd" who died to give them life and that more abundantly than they had ever known before. Throughout the years, I have had many roles in my life—as a parent, as a wife, as a foster parent, as a poet, as a clown, as a minister. I performed weddings, funerals, and church services, but I've discovered that what I have done, or what I do, does not define me. In all my roles in life, I have had one purpose, to be like Jesus and to serve with joy!

What defines me is my relationship with Jesus. That's where I find peace—and why not? He is the Prince of Peace! Life throws a lot of curves our way, but when we become intimately acquainted with Jesus, who is the Way, the Truth, and the Life, we're in far greater hands, and that's a much better insurance policy. Our choices are unending, and steadfast perseverance is more easily attained by making the right choices and obtaining the reward! In Philippians 3:13–14, Paul wrote: "Brethren, I do not count myself to have apprehended; but one thing I do, forgetting those things which are behind and reaching forward to those things which are ahead, I press toward the goal for the prize of the upward call of God in Christ Jesus." This, too, has been my quest. My testimony isn't as much in my past as it is in my future! It's important to focus on your end, not your beginning. Your response determines your outcome.

There's a reality I want to talk to you about, but it's never very pleasant, and most of us really don't want to think about it; nonetheless, it's true! We will live forever—either with God or separated from Him for eternity. It was never God's plan for man to be in hell! I implore you to seek Jesus Christ today and follow Him for the rest of your life. Peace only comes through believing and following the Word of God.

Rewards of Overcoming Lawlessness

Hell was created for the devil and his angels, but if you're not serving God, whether you agree or not, like it or not, you are serving the devil! There's no middle of the road here. In the New Testament, Jesus said, "The thief does not come except to steal, and to kill, and to destroy. I have come that they may have life, and that they may have it more abundantly" (John 10:10). Hell is not the place where God wants you to end up. When Jesus took your sin upon the cross, He also went to hell. He took the keys to hell and death so that He could legally purchase life for us for eternity. He told us that in His Father's house there are many mansions. He has gone to prepare a place for us so that where He is, we may be also.

Because of medical breakthroughs and modern technology, many people have been brought back from the dead with shock paddles, and some have documented their experiences when this took place. Some have gone toward a bright light and experienced a glimpse of heaven while others folded into the deep darkness, terrorized, experiencing excruciating pain and unbearable torment! All their senses were fully intact, and they were able to see, touch, smell, speak, and hear, magnified intensely over what they had known on the earth. Tangible deep darkness enveloped them, and worms, spiders, and demonic creatures never before seen tormented them.

They experienced the stench of burning, rotting flesh, the odor of putrid sulfur, and horrific screams of torment echoed from prison chambers clamoring with chains of bondage!

Many of those people brought back to life were astounded and felt they had been greatly deceived because they thought they were going to heaven when they died. They thought they were good, that their good deeds outweighed their bad. Many of them had professed to be Christians, but there was never a DNA change in their heart. God knows your heart, and you know your heart needs to change from who you are to who God created you to be/ Jesus said, "You must be born again." You must lose your old life (burying the old nature) in baptism and rise to newness of life in Him! He said, "If you love Me, you'll obey Me!" He tells us not to fail to assemble ourselves together in His name. To be an active part of the Body, we must connect to others and function as a vital part of His Body, loving, serving, and meeting with each other, understanding that it is no longer our life, but His! It has been bought and paid for with a price! If we freely have given our lives to Him, then we need to get off the throne of our lives and put Him there!

Paul shows us how important it is to know God and accept Him. While Paul was in rebellion and slaughtering Christians, because he was a Pharisee as touching the Law, his religious convictions made him one of the most unlikely instruments to be used by God. On the other hand, his conversion was a powerful testimony to his witness of Jesus Christ. This conversion occurred on the road to Damascus as he was blinded by the light of Christ, and this act signifies a critical point in the history of Christianity. God called to Paul to use him as a vessel to spread the Word of Jesus Christ, who is the Light of the world. John 1 says the *light* of Christ came into the world, but the world loved the darkness more than the *light*. I encourage you to read Acts 9, concerning the calling of Paul by God. God planned a divine intervention for Paul, and for a time the *light* worked through the darkness in Paul's theology. The *light* exposed the darkness, and the truth set Paul free! When God's messenger finally reached Paul, he was no longer blind, but totally sold out to not only reaching for the prize but reaching others to see and know the truth as well!

God had a purpose for Paul, which was to proclaim that Jesus was Savior and Lord. When I think of Paul and his teachings, I stand in awe that God used him thousands of years ago to reach the Gentiles, and his teachings are still used today to bring the Word of Jesus Christ to a lost people. God wants His family to grow, and He wants you to get onboard and follow your destiny, which includes becoming a spiritual part of God's family.

Family

A master vessel was designed with craftsmanship and skill,
A vessel bound for glory by the navigator's will.

There's no doubt the vessel's worthy;
There's no doubt she'll stand the storm.

She's been deemed as indestructible from fury, rage, or harm.
But she carries precious cargo, there be treasures in her hold.

And the pirates aim to steal away and loot the jewels and gold,
So, a plan came to the Master's mind, this be what He'll do.

To bring an overseer onboard to call and train a crew,
So the crew came by their powers, strong to suit their trade.

Diverse and yet amazingly equipped to earn what they are paid,
Even so as a *whisper* blows, these mates have fixed their sights.

Their differences have raised the brow
like strangers in the night.
They gather at their places to cluster where they shine.

Insensitive as needs may be to passers of the time,
Let's pipe the skipper aboard, mates, and cast us out to sea.

Let's bring this vessel honor, with our crew called FAMILY.
For there stands a new horizon, a calm beyond the blue.

Hail to the Chief, our awesome God,
And bless His stately crew.

Inspired by the Captain of the Storm,
Faun Collett

Prayer

Father, You are greater than life and worthy of much more than we can give, but we lift our hearts to You in love and adoration! You are amazing and a wonder to behold. I am so very blessed that You are mindful of me. Even in this imperfect dimension, Your grace and loving-kindness cover me by the saving blood of the Lamb, who has blotted out my sin. It is by my power and not by my might, but entirely by Your Holy Spirit. As I reflect on this earthly journey with You walking hand in hand, I am mindful of the delight Adam had with You in the cool of the evening, and even more so of the unlimited access I have to You because Your Spirit has no limitations on Your time allotted to me. You are the Vine, and I am the branch that gets to be fed and matured to bring glory to Your name. For this purpose is the Son of God made manifest, to destroy the works of the evil one. What a beautiful legacy we have to bring to Your glory. Amen.

Notes

Notes

Chapter 6

Deliver Us from Evil

The Bible gives us the following message: "Then He will also say to those on the left hand, 'Depart from Me, you cursed, into the everlasting fire prepared for the devil and his angels'" (Matthew 25:41).

Early in *The Jesus Whisperer,* I discussed a truth that I want to reiterate concerning our choices in life and the choices we make about the live hereafter. For many people, the topic of hell is not pleasurable, and many of us really don't want to even think about it. When we think about hell, we need to consider our choices; after all, whether you or I go to heaven or to hell is a matter of our personal choice. Simply put, we will live forever, either with God or separated from Him for eternity.

The Need for Humility

In the Church, many pastors or ministers discuss the importance of humility; because we tend to have a sinful nature, we should be willing to examine our pride and focus on being humble so we can serve our heavenly Father, who showers us with mercy and grace. To sum up what my pastor always taught us: Humility is the ability to receive what you will never deserve! We are changed by what we know! The Bible says that you shall know the truth (Jesus), and the truth shall set you free. He whom the Son sets free is free, indeed! It is the goodness of God that leads us to change our hearts and minds, so, "Teach me to do Your will, for You are my God; Your Spirit is good. Lead me in the land of uprightness" (Psalm 143:10). We cannot enter heaven without Jesus Christ, and we must practice humility and surrender our hearts to God's will. It is not by our power or might, but by God's Spirit that produces change as we give Him permission to invade our space and honor Him.

The apostle Paul wrote, "For all have sinned and fall short of the glory of God" (Romans 3:23). Most of us do not like to think about what lies ahead, or when or how we will die. But there is a fact that is unavoidable and that is that we are all going to die. God *whispers* to us, extending to us an invitation to know Him and to ask for forgiveness for our sins. He wants us to come to Him and live with Him forever. However, uncountable numbers of people will deny Him and simply say, "I don't believe this is the right thing for me, God!" That's what my wicked nature naturally says, and that's what yours says too! Our natural defiance is to sin (miss the mark), and it's our greatest burden. I encourage you to read the poem "Miss the Mark" again, because it is something everyone has done in their life.

We must learn to arm ourselves for the fight of faith. One of the best illustrations I ever heard was of the boxer who left the comfort of his home to enter a training camp. He was on a very strict diet, drank raw eggs every morning, worked out, and ran many miles a day to build his endurance. In addition, he sparred hour after hour in the ring with his fellow boxers. He listened to his coach and sacrificed on a daily basis everything he could in order to condition himself for the day of the championship fight. Finally, the day of the fight arrived, and he went into the ring, met his opponent, and fought with all his might. His opponent had not been idle, but he was filled with hate and bent on destruction, pounding blow after blow into this boxer.

By the time the ten rounds were up, this boxer had been beaten and bruised almost beyond recognition. His eyes were swollen shut and had to be slit in order for him to see. His body was pulverized, but in the last round, he knocked out his opponent cold. He won the title of world champion, and they put a huge belt around him, held up his hands, and presented him to his fans. Then they took him to the back, patched him up, cleaned him up, and rubbed him down while the manager approached him with a check for the victory he had won. With a check for thousands of dollars, he headed home, and his beautiful wife met him at the door, where he gave her the check.

In the end, he fought the fight, won the prize, and turned it over to his wife. Do you know what that makes her? He was the conqueror, but she was *more* than a conqueror, because all she had to do was be married to him and receive what he worked so hard to achieve for her. *That is exactly what Jesus did for us!* He left the comfort of His home (heaven), laid down His deity, and fought His opponent. He won the fight, took the keys of hell and death, and freely gave them to us, His Bride. All we have to do is receive His provision and great love. *What a victory, what a deal!* When I think about the keys to hell and death, I think about an elderly man I once knew named Fred. Fred was a rebel when it came to accepting God in his life. Fortunately for Fred, and before his death, he called on God for forgiveness and asked Him to come dwell in his heart.

Lord, Here's Fred

Lord, here's Fred! He came to me at ninety-two years young.

His mind was strong, but as he talked,

he fought back shedding tears.

Decade after decade, this man wandered on his own.

He had some ups and faced some downs,

but now Fred feels alone.

Don't get me wrong—his family has been a great reward,

And Fred has always taken pride in working very hard.

But not too long ago, Lord, as we took the time to chat,

Fred told me he was very lost and not sure where he's at.

He said he had a need for God, and wanted to believe,

But religion built some doctrines he couldn't quite receive.

He felt that he was honest when he turned his back on You

And chose to walk away from all the rules You'd hold him to.

Forgive him, Lord, he didn't know that all he had to lose

Were lies the devil told to him, and singing hopeless blues.

He didn't know that all the glitter Satan tries to sell

Would steal true life away from him, and send a man to hell.

He said he didn't understand, and now he has regrets,
Because I shared the beauty of how Jesus cancelled debts.
It wasn't something Fred could do, to pay his price of sin.
Jesus paid that long ago, but Fred must be born again.

I told him grace was never earned, Your favor never wanes,
That Jesus wants to wipe his tears and take away his pains.
And, Lord, Fred prayed with me that day
and asked if You would come
To meet with him and reveal Yourself,
in the Person of Your Son.

It's still hard for Fred to see, how after all this time
You'd want this old and withered man,
and bade him come and dine,
But he took the invitation to eternal life and joy.
Dear Lord, for just a moment, precious Fred looked like a boy!

A smile appeared on old Fred's face; the worry seemed to go.
Ancient of Days, meet my friend Fred.
There's so much he wants to know.
I'm glad we took the time to talk—it wasn't very hard—
For my friend, Fred, has seen the Light,
and now Jesus is his Lord.

Inspired by the need to pray,
Faun Collett

Fred was ninety-two years old and very ill. He was rushed to the hospital on a cold winter night, and my prayer partner drove over forty miles in one of the worst ice storms we had ever had to pray and again attempt to tell him about Jesus. On her way to the hospital, she called and asked me to be in prayer. As I began to intercede, these words came to me and I wrote the poem down. Later, I was told that Fred accepted Jesus that night, just as I had written in the poem. God is such an awesome, patient, and loving Friend, and He waits with outstretched arms to embrace all who come to Him.

The Bible says that we are *more than conquerors through Jesus Christ,* who loves us, and we have been given the ultimate victory, but we must labor to enter into God's rest. So, my words to you are these! Remember that the Bible is the infallible Word of God and that all things must be filtered through its pages! Rick, Blake, Ava, Krissy, Liam, Seamus, Sloane, and any unknown grandchildren who may be coming after I'm gone, you know I love you, and to all my family and friends, I pray blessings upon you all! And finally, this I shout from the heavens: Know God, read the Word, serve with joy, finish strong, and hurry home! I encourage you to seek and accept Jesus Christ.

A Poetic Message to
My Loved Ones.

My darling daughter,

I wanted to write a Christmas Poem......one that doesn't rhyme. One expressing so much more than I can begin to say with flowery words or wit. Sometimes those things that rhyme loose their true expression as the focus turns from what you want to convey with style to flowery words instead of substance, which I so deeply hope to convey. I hope you hear the cry of my heart. In just this last year alone, you have been a blazing torch through a very physically challenging but healing journey. You have extended yourself with deep thought, consideration and great effort to lighten my load. The Hovearound has been a God send in more ways than you could know; it has helped me conserve energy as I navigate my way around a beautiful octagon home. It has given me a freedom to cruise round this anointed land and reflect in prayer, and it has helped restore my soul.

When I open my eyes in the morning, I know I will find in each new day a loving phone call inquiring of my needs and letting me know you are just around the corner. When I lost so much weight and went from a size 2X to a woman's size 14, you were on it like a honey bee with sweet blooms ahead. Before I could bat my eyes, I had a new wardrobe for casual and dress. I never expected you to provide what you have, but your thoughtfulness just doesn't quit. When my physical battle with stage four lung cancer had weakened my body, and I couldn't get out of bed, you prayed for me and faithfully attended my Christmas shopping, making sure my presents were ordered and wrapped in time for Christmas. WOW, with all you had to do with taking care of your family, work, and decorating your new country home for our Upcoming Family Country Christmas and planning our Christmas meal, you completely took care of your Momma.

You have made a lasting impression on my oncologist who says you have a good head on your shoulders, and she's absolutely right! A head that is always thinking in advance to make things better for your world. With your gifts, you continue to bless your children, your family, friends, your neighbors and their lives. I can't keep up with the you, you do, and very, very little times goes to taking care of you.

When I close my eyes at night, for just a few short, peaceful moments, I reflect on Blue Ridge Mountain Down Home adventure. You choose the most perfect family adventure with all of the trimmings. The hot tub, my waterfall shower, the awesome lookout deck, the display of flocks of turkey, deer, and even a curious bear briefly visit me and remind me of the blessings that have overtaken me. WOW, what an awesome storehouse of memories you have afforded us. All I can say is my dear darling, outstanding daughter, you light up my life, and I hope I can wrap up 2021 with the real and awesome Christmas you have given me, the Gift of YOU. Merry Christmas Kisssy.

Love Momma

Christy

When you came into my life,
Your life flooded into me
You were such a blessing and serendipity
Your giftings and your caring ways
Was a step above the rest
And I knew that God had gifted me
With nothing but His best
You are always in our moments
And your presences passes time
Just saying "Yes" your father, Doug
Has also made you mine
In some small way to parent you
Withstood the test of time
Unwrapping you as a step daughter
Has simply been sublime
And Curtis is the sweetest icing
On all you say and do
And praying His blessings in 2022
I'm thanking God for the priceless gift of you

Love, Mama Faun

Liam, My First Grand Love

Liam Joseph Moylan
How Blessed I am to say
The very mention of your name
Brightens up my day

The first time your mommy told me
You were waiting to arrive
I thought you were the greatest thing
To ever grace my life

I couldn't wait to see you
And to look into your eyes
To love you and to hold you
And to smile at my surprise

To sing to you and rock you
While I watched you go to sleep
As you snuggled deep into my chest
I could feel your little heart beat

And with every beat that pounded
So closely to my heart
I knew no matter where you were
We'd never be apart

Because you were my first grandchild
You will always be to me
The beginning of Grand blessings
Climbing on our family tree

Though each grandchild is special
And each one sent from God above
Liam Joseph Moylan
You're the first of all I Love

by Grandma Faun

Seamus, One Like No Other

Seamus, you have filled my heart
With more than Love and Joy
You've been a treasure sent from God
And you're an awesome man-child boy

These years are filled with wonder
Your life is full and good
You have the best to offer
And you've given all you could

I remember when you were a toddler
How busy you would be
When you stuck your finger in the door
And you were hurt severely

I prayed you would recover
And you recovered well
When one day you found yourself
Again in the midst of hell

That same finger that was hurt
Was healing up so nice
When you stuck it in a buggy spoke
And it was cut off, damaged twice

I was in Missouri then
When I got that horrible call
And prayed again with your mother
As she took you from that fall.

I told her not to worry
You can't walk in faith and fear
Only God could intervene
And bring healing here

We stormed the gates of heaven
And we believed He'd do His part
To turn the evil deed around
And protect your little heart

Your finger was reattached
Through a surgeon's skill
And you recovered with incredible speed
Because we prayed God's Will

I know you've faced some challenges
And I'm sorry for every bruise
But I know that God is faithful
When He is who you choose

I hope that every battle
That ever comes your way
Will only empower you to overcome
When you take the time to pray

Seamus, you're a winner in my books
You're the apple of my eye
And I hope your dreams enable you
To reach beyond the sky

Because the sky is not the limit
Nothing can stop your destiny
If you resist all fear and resistance
And recognize your enemy

You're more than a conqueror
And made to rule and reign
I couldn't be prouder of who you are
And I wish you success and fame

I hope you always remember
You're in my heart and prayers
No matter when or where I go
I'll always keep you there

I love you more than you may know
I love every part of you
Seamus my middle Grand son
I'm so Blessed that you are you

(And I'm so proud of what you do)

Love Grandma Faun
Merry Christmas 2021

"Sloane"

Sloane, your feminine name in Irish
A Sweet little raider you be
And your demeanor brought invasion
To our active family

You showed up at the perfect time
When the family needed more
God knew you would meet that need
When He brought you to our door.

A perfect little raider
With wisdom deep inside
We knew we'd been invaded
And we loved your bubbly side

With a family full of fellows
And a need for feminine grace
You were the gift God gave to us
And your sweetness set the pace

Everything about you
Makes this Grandma smile
And every moment with you
Makes my life worthwhile

You fill my days with sunshine
You chase away my tears
I know the time will come dear one
When days will turn to years

When that designated time comes
I hope you stand in faith
And step up on the battle field
Where you can take my place

Fight the fight with vigor
Jesus is your friend
Faith will hold you firmly
Knowing you will win

And I know all I came to do
Will decorate your shield with power
To overcome the battles
As you triumph in this hour

You're such an overcomer
You conquer every test
Remember how I love you
And Enjoy God's Very Best

Love Grandma Faun
And Grandpa Doug too

Blake Daniel

Little Blake Daniel it's amazing to me

That Jesus would place you on our family tree

Surrounded with love

Bundled with care

Swaddled with tenderness

Covered in prayer

Even the leaves

that have fallen with age

Are singing about you with colorful praise

Our Heavenly Father

blessed us beyond measure

By gifting our family with such

Priceless treasure

With kisses and hugs

We cherish your light

And can't wait to see

What you do with your life

We'll never forsake you

Or leave you alone

We'll always be with you

When thoughts turn to home

So sleep little baby in the tree top

You're incredibly awesome and you totally rock

My Darling Ava

Ava, your name means Eve
And a perfect name to call
My last grand baby girl was sent
To fill my days with awe

I love you more than flowers
I love you more than stars
I loved you even before you came
More than Jupiter and Mars

You are so very special
Even tho' you're far away
I think of you unending
You're the sparkle in my day

I am so blessed to have a little girl
Who is kind and sweet and smart
You have made my life so beautiful
You are right here in my heart

And if you ever miss me
I hope you always know
My love and prayers are with you
As you develop and grow

I thank God for my treasure

Such a perfect gift you are

And you'll always shine much brighter

Than any distant star

I love you every morning

And when the day is done

You're my perfect little Angel

And the trophy of my son

Remember that I love you

Beyond the galaxies

And will treasure you throughout all times

In my heart and on my knees

Ava, since you are my last grandchild, I wrote one more poem for you to grow on.

AVA

My darling, priceless granddaughter,
How can I count the ways?
You have brightened up my life
With your sweet and loving praise.

Every time I see you,
Every smile and hug and kiss
Fills me with thanksgiving
As I go to reminisce.

You're a little blue-eyed wonder;
No wonder you're so smart.
Filled with so much sweetness,
We will never be apart.

You were the icing on the cake,
My gift from heaven above.
I'll cherish you to infinity,
Beyond all the numbers you are loved.

Because each time I think of you,
And each time you remember me,
We'll think about our special times,
And our love will last eternally.

—*Grandma Faun and Grandpa Doug, too*

Comfort That Only Jesus Christ Can Provide

How comforting to realize that I am not alone, and that whatever comes my way is no surprise to Jesus. He does no evil, but He gives me great comfort, power, and victory to overcome all of my challenges. I know my battle is *not* against flesh and blood, and I can now see things in a new perspective and fight the powers, principalities, and rulers of darkness and wickedness in heavenly places. Because I know who I am in Christ, I put on the armor provided for me, I take up the sword of God (the Word), and I bind and loose with authority, my adversaries must flee from me.

Having a relationship with Jesus and knowing the Word has given me great peace and the tools to win every battle. The New Testament tells us this: "Therefore gird up the loins of your mind, be sober, and rest your hope fully upon the grace that is to be brought to you at the revelation of Jesus Christ; as obedient children, not conforming yourselves to the former lusts, as in your ignorance; but as He who called you is holy, you also be holy in all your conduct, because it is written, 'Be holy, for I am holy'" (1 Peter 1:13–16). The weapons we need to fight our battles are not the weapons of the world, but they are the weapons God has given to us through His written Word. God has the divine *power* that we need to demolish strongholds. We demolish arguments and *every* thought that sets itself up against the knowledge of

God. We are to take captive every thought to make it obedient to Christ, and we must be ready to punish every act of disobedience once our obedience is complete. Even now, as I approach the end of my earthly walk, I am learning to take authority as a believer more than ever before. I desire to rule and reign in my realm of influence by walking in love, praying in the Spirit (1 Corinthians 12–14), and *glorifying God,* thus fulfilling my destiny in my generation. Being filled with the Holy Spirit has taken me to a whole new level in Christ, and it is a path I would never sidestep. Jesus is now sitting at the right hand of the Father; He said before He ascended that it was expedient that He should go so the Holy Spirit could come. I would never want to be any place where the Holy Spirit was not welcome. He is the One here on earth now, and He came to give me *power.* Acts 1:8 tells us, "But you shall receive power when the Holy Spirit has come upon you...." God will never forsake His followers, and He will provide us with the power we need to complete the tasks our heavenly Father has set before us.

Simply Believe

The Lord made it so simple, explaining clearly who He was, but the people just wouldn't believe. The veil over their eyes, ears, and heart hindered their ability to hear beyond the natural, but He is a supernatural God. So, what does it take to hear His voice? Simply believe. In Matthew 16:24, Jesus said to His disciples, "If anyone desires to come after Me, let him deny himself, and take up his cross, and follow Me." I encourage you to take the step of faith and believe on Jesus Christ, because He is the Truth and the Way to eternal life.

The book of 1 John reveals "who is he that overcomes the world, but he who believes that Jesus is the Son of God?" Verse 6 reveals who He is: "This is He who came by water and blood—Jesus Christ; not only by water, but by water and blood. [He did not come by water only, but by water and blood.] And it is the Spirit who bears witness, because the Spirit is truth." Verse 7 reveals the unity God desires: "For there are three...the Father, the Word, and the Holy Spirit; and these three are one." And in verse 8, we see the message that "... there are three that bear witness on earth: the Spirit, the water, and the blood; and these three agree as one" (1 John 5:5–8). Believe the Father, believe the Word, and believe the Holy Spirit. The Father sent the Son, the Son sent the Holy Spirit, and the three are one. They agree–and so should we.

Earlier in this book, I testified of hearing His voice, telling me to pray for the eighty-six-year-old woman who had been declared dead, and then later, He spoke while I was walking down a road praying. He told me to knock on a door three houses away from where I was. To report each time I heard His voice would take seventy years of transcripts. Unfortunately, I didn't always obey, and many times I doubted. When Jesus promised the Holy Spirit, He made this statement: "If you love Me, keep My commandments. And I will pray the Father, and He will give you another Helper, that He may abide with you forever—the Spirit of truth, whom the world cannot receive, because it neither sees Him nor knows Him; but you know Him, for He dwells with you and will be in you" (John 14:15–17). Our God is so kind, loving, and forgiving toward us, and after seventy years on earth, I still find unspeakable joy in walking in the garden of His love, waiting for His *whispering* voice and sharing His loving-kindness with all who will hear.

Sharing God's Mercy and Grace

As I consider my obligation to share God's Word with those I meet during my life's journey, I am reminded of meeting Father Mike and Patrick. This was not a meeting of chance, but it was a meeting directed by God. Oftentimes we think of meeting up with others as an everyday event that brings no personal value to our lives. However, many times God puts people in our lives, and we need to recognize them as gifts from our heavenly Father. Perhaps we do not always look at an encounter with a stranger as a gift, but many times they are the ones who bless us, even when we do not recognize the purpose behind God's plan. A chance meeting with a stranger may provide an opportunity for you to share the message of God's love and salvation, or it may simply mean that God wants to enrich your life with the presence of others.

Father Mike and St. John's Parish

One day when Doug and I went to Jersey Mike's to get a sandwich, an elderly man was there, wearing a black shirt and black pants. He was with a younger man, and after the elderly man walked past me twice and then went to sit down, I walked over to him and said, "You look really familiar to me. You're a priest, aren't you?" He was not wearing a collar, but he *was* wearing a necklace that I had seen priests wear as part of their attire. He was surprised I could tell he was a priest, because he wasn't wearing his collar. Our brief comments quickly turned into quite a conversation! He told me his name was Father Mike and that he was a priest at St. John's Parish on Twenty-Sixth Street. He asked what parish I was from, and I replied that I didn't have a parish—but that I was not perishing! He laughed; and I asked if I could tell him a story. When he agreed, I sat at his table, which he was sharing with the young man, Patrick, who was thirty-five.

I shared the story about the eighty-six-year-old woman whom God had raised from the dead after my prayer. The priest asked if I spoke in tongues, and when I replied, "Yes, I do," he said, "That is so interesting. You're not here by accident! Yesterday, we were talking about how the Holy Spirit doesn't get much focus—and that the Holy Spirit is doing a work here." He said that he also spoke in tongues, then he asked if I knew that God had sent me there that day. That started a long conversation, during which Doug finished his meal, and we had such beautiful fellowship. At the end of our time together, the priest said, "I have to have your phone number. You are very anointed, and God has a very special call on your life." He asked us to pray for him and Patrick. He placed my hand on Patrick, and then he took my other hand and told me that Patrick had been diagnosed with Parkinson's disease. So, I prayed for Patrick: "Father, I pray that Patrick lives out every day that You have ordained for him to live on this earth and that he fulfills his destiny." Later, I would learn that Patrick had been brought to the priest's door by a custodian. He had all kinds of issues, including a serious heart problem, and his health was declining rapidly.

During our time of fellowship at Jersey Mike's, the conversation turned to healing, and the priest asked, "Will you pray with me?" I told him that I would pray in agreement with him. I usually pray for people only when they ask me to do so, but I felt the Lord wanted me to do something different for Patrick. So, I asked Patrick if I could lay hands on him. When he said, "yes," I laid my hands on Patrick and asked him to be in agreement when I prayed. We needed to know the Word and stand on the Word. I told Patrick that we had to fight the fight of faith, that it was not a dance. We overcome by the Lamb and the word of our testimony. I said to Patrick, "You have a testimony, and the biggest distance in the world is the distance between your head and your heart." As I touched his chest, I told him, "God wants you to declare and decree, to rule and to reign with all the authority that has been given to us by the Word of God." I prayed for him, but I also told him that he needed to declare every day that sickness is not of God. He was to reject it and fight against it, claiming the truth that Jesus had died and paid the price for his healing and his life.

Afterward, Father Mike asked me to pray for him because he had a driver's test the next day; if he did not pass the test, he would not be able to take Patrick to doctor appointments and to the other places he needed to go. So, I prayed for him and asked him to agree that our covenant-keeping God would honor our request and that healing would be his portion, in Jesus' name.

Father Mike was awestruck. I told him about my writings on *The Two Sides of the Mountain,* and he was so blessed by that. He he knew our meeting was definitely ordained, a divine appointment, that I was sent by God and had a mighty calling. He asked again if he could call me, and I told him, "Anytime." At the end, I told him disease was not a part of his covenant with God, and that included Patrick's diagnosis of Parkinson's disease.

Keep in mind that God may also put *you* in a place of need. He may want you to stand in the gap so you can introduce someone else to the Father, Son, and Holy Spirit. If this is your calling in such a time as this, don't let it pass you by. Remember that God wants to expand his heavenly family, and you may be just the messenger needed to share the Word of God with a new citizen of heaven.

Prophetic Messages

As you read the prophetic messages below, I pray that you will accept the message of Jesus Christ and invite Him into your life. He is waiting for you and longing for you to call out to Him.

> *As a citizen of heaven:* I will declare the goodness of God here on the earth. Although I can't wrap my mind around everything I read in the Bible, I believe it is infallible and 100 percent true. Jesus is seated in the heavenly places. The book of Ephesians tells us: "And God raised us up

with Christ and seated us with Him in the heavenly realms in Christ Jesus" (Ephesians 2:6 NIV). That means I can rule and reign from that place right now, declaring and decreeing His will on this earth be done even as it is in heaven, and being an extension of His hands, feet, and body. I am His temple, and He abides in me and I in Him. I can hear His voice, and so can you, if you'll take Him at His Word and only believe.

Scars and wounds: The Lord says: *"This is the time when I'll uncover the scars and wounds and the things that have festered. I'll uncover them with mercy and wash them with Your waters of life! I will scrape away the scabs and ugly things, and I will reveal newness, restoration, hope, and destination. Yield yourself as I sculpt your beauty from within and I mold you into My Son. Then and only then will My glory fill all the earth. Commune with Me, love your community, and reconcile with others. Love them and bring them back to Me. Cover them, and My Kingdom will come and bring so much more—more love, more peace, more joy, and more of Me!"*

Hear My voice: The Lord says: *"Do you suppose I would give antennas to the ants to sensitize their hearing, but leave you, who has been fashioned in My image and likeness, without insight and foresight? Hear this: All of My creation has the ability to hear My voice. The mountains, the rivers, the valleys, and the trees of the field shall clap their hands! The nations will hear Me and see Me as veiled, but I am not hidden from you! You are My chosen one, the one to whom*

I choose to demonstrate the mystery of the figs through and by My Spirit, which I have placed within you, providing you with far more than the wisdom of Solomon. I have given you the mind of Christ! Seek Me with all of your heart, and I will cause you to see, hear, and taste My goodness. Then I will serve the world through you."

In this you greatly rejoice, though now for a little while, if need be, you have been grieved by various trials, that the genuineness of your faith, being much more precious than gold that perishes, though it is tested by fire, may be found to praise, honor, and glory at the revelation of Jesus Christ.

—1 Peter 1:6

Prayer

God Loves You

God loves you, and He wants you to know Him in order to fill you with peace and give you real life—forever. "God loved the people of this world so much that He gave His only Son, so that everyone who has faith in Him will have eternal life and never die." Jesus also said, "I came so that everyone would have life, and have it in its fullest." Because God planned for us to have peace and life, why are we then so far from God? I encourage you to pray this simple prayer with total surrender and trust"

The Prayer for Salvation

Dear heavenly Father, I come to You in the name above every name, Jesus. Lord Jesus, thank You for dying for my sins. Please come into my life and make me new in You . Forgive me for my sins and wash me by You redeeming blood. Holy Spirit, I invite You to fill me, instruct me, guide me, and lead me home. In Jesus' name, amen.

Notes

Chapter 7

God Will Not Forsake Us

"Behold, I am the LORD, the God of all flesh. Is there anything too hard for Me?"

—Jeremiah 32:27

God desires a relationship with us. Through prayer, we communicate with the One who knows us completely and who loves us perfectly. Prayer is two-way communication, in which we not only speak to Him, but He also speaks to us—and sometimes it is in a quiet *whisper*.

Trying to work and go to school proved to be too much for me, and I had a breakdown and returned home defeated. I found a job as a floor instructor at a health spa, and while I was there, I met the man who would be my next husband and the father of my two wonderful children. Rick was born in 1970, and four years later in May, Chrissy, the most beautiful baby girl who ever lived on the earth, completed my joy. For the first time, I felt like I had done something right because my children were my whole world and raising them right was my greatest ambition.

Their father and I were together for seventeen years, and we built a home in St. Peters, Missouri. We raised our family there, in a neighborhood that was amazing for the children. Many relationships were written on our hearts in that wonderland of forever friends. Sadly, our marriage failed, and afterward, I became self-absorbed, desperately trying to make it in a world that seemed unrelenting and cruel. During those hard times, God became my strength and song. I watched Him intervene to provide for us more times than I could count, and my church family became my shield, loving me, encouraging me, and cheering me on. I cleaned doctors' houses, worked at preschools as a music teacher, and drove a school bus to bring in our provisions, and God did the rest.

My children rarely saw a doctor, because if they ever got sick, I laid hands on them and prayed and received instant results. One day, little Ricky had a fever of 106! He was just a young baby, and I was a new mother, but I called a minister on the phone who told me to lay my hands on Rick while he prayed. Ricky cooled off so fast that I pulled my hand away in shock—the fever broke instantly! I discovered the power of the name of Jesus and prayer. It was the same for my daughter, Chrissy. Sickness was not something that stayed in our household very long.

In school, both Rick and Chris were honor students, with perfect attendance almost all the way through school, and they were extremely good children most of the time. They set their own clocks to get up in the morning, and they worked hard, played hard, and were extremely disciplined. Of course, they had their moments of stubbornness, but overall they accepted correction and were quick to adjust and make the right decisions. I was so proud of them both, I was so blessed to have had the privilege of raising them during that very short time of their childhoods. The time flew by faster than I realized!

After each of them graduated from high school, they worked very hard to put themselves through college with little help from me, as I had nothing I could give to them financially. Just taking care of the house and car payments, insurance, utilities, and living expenses was all I could handle. My children had suffered the horrors of a broken home, and they had to fend for themselves in many ways, but I believed the foundation God gave me to instill in them would outlast the downfalls, and I faithfully prayed they would prosper and achieve success along with see God's divine protection upon their lives.

Finding Strength through Faith

During my divorce, there came a point and time in my life when I decided to study to become an EKG technician, and I went to apply at vocational rehabilitation school. After a battery of tests, I went into the school's office, where the counselor told me that if my IQ were two points lower, I wouldn't be a plant, I'd be a rock. Because of my financial situation and my physical limitations, he told me I qualified for educational benefits, but that I would never make it and I should just forget about schooling because my test results indicated I would never succeed. I left his office devastated, but only for a few minutes. Then it dawned on me that I was in a spiritual battle and the devil was trying to rob me of my future.

Many times we never realize we are in a spiritual battle, but I could see clearly that this was an all-out attack to send me back home without hope. The devil is a liar, and instead of getting depressed and defeated, a righteous indignation came upon me. I stopped in the hallway and said, "Devil, you're a liar, and I bind you from your deceptions. I'm the head and not the foot, above and not beneath. I have the mind of Christ, and I can do all things through Christ who strengthens me. So get behind me in the name of Jesus!" I went back inside and told the man that I wanted to enroll at Forest Park Community College. I took the EKG course, passed with all Bs, and then went to Barnes Hospital, St. Louis, to finish my required studies and training with straight As.

We often find ourselves in spiritual battles that can only be won with spiritual weapons. In the Bible, Jesus said, "Because of your unbelief; for assuredly, I say to you, if you have faith as a mustard seed, you will say to this mountain, 'Move from here to there,' and it will move; and nothing will be impossible for you" (Matthew 17:20). Faith in God and the knowledge of the Word of God, along with the name of Jesus and the power of the Holy Spirit, provides us with the will to fight the fight of faith. At that time, the Word of God, which I had been reading for years, finally kicked in and helped me to be as *bold* as a lion. My faith increased as I practiced walking out the Word and building a relationship with my Savior! In Isaiah 41.10, the words of God comfort the believer: "Fear not, for I am with you; be not dismayed, for I am your God. I will strengthen you. Yes, I will help you,

I will uphold you with My righteous right hand." Because of my faith in God, the Son, and the Holy Spirit, I have seen more miracles than I could begin to count—all because I simply believed!

Raising the Dead

One day in 1985, I was at work as a medical technician performing routine EKGs. Suddenly "Code Blue—Emergency Room" bellowed over the hospital loudspeaker. I ran to the ER, grabbed a crash cart, and hooked up an elderly lady who'd had a heart attack at her home and was brought in by ambulance. Although the EMTs had worked on her, along with the medical team in the ER, she never regained a heart rhythm, and after a half hour, the lead doctor called her time of death. The nurse charted the time, and everyone left the ER except for me. When I went over to disconnect the monitor from her body, God spoke to me as clearly as I'm speaking to you now, except I didn't hear Him audibly—I heard Him in my spirit. He told me that if I didn't pray for her, she would spend eternity separated from Him.

I was shocked for a number of reasons. First, just hearing God's voice was awe-inspiring, but equally awesome was the fact that God would ask me to pray for this woman at her time of death. *I immediately told Him I would not only pray for her, but that if He brought her back, I would tell her what happened.* I laid my hands on her and commanded life into her body in the name of Jesus. When I looked up at the monitor, I saw that her heart had started beating. Talk about a rush! I immediately ran into the hall and called back the medical team; before long I was pushed back in the corner while they all worked over her again. They thought they were making a difference and had no idea what had just happened.

Later, before the woman was discharged from the hospital, I went into her room to perform another routine EKG. I asked her if she knew what had happened the day they brought her to the hospital. She told me they'd said she'd died, but she didn't remember anything. I told her how God had told me to pray for her lest she spend eternity separated from Him. She looked at me in shock. She had rejected God all of her life and never allowed anyone to talk to her about God or invite her to church.

This woman wanted nothing to do with God because of something that had happened to her when she was young—but she couldn't understand why God would want anything to do with her now, as an old woman. I told her it was not God's choice to be separated from her, that He had paid a great price for her so she could be with Him forever—but it was her choice. With tears in her eyes, she asked what she should do. I helped her to pray a simple prayer, asking for forgiveness of her sins and receiving Jesus as her Savior, and I left her hospital room filled with the love and presence of God.

Although I never saw her again and don't even know her name, I look forward to the day when we meet again in heaven. I was so moved and blessed by this dear soul. She had weathered many challenges in her lifetime, without the presence of God to lift the burdens that so troubled her. I wrote the following poem to express God's mercy and grace, and share how He intervened in the life of one of His lost sheep:

Raising the Dead

She looked so isolated
As they rushed her through the door.
Her frail, thin body motionless
On the emergency room floor.

From the gurney to the table,
Underneath a massive light,
The ER staff and doctors
Began fighting for her life.

With all the latest instruments
And machines to aid their task,
Every trained technician
Worked skillfully and fast.

Time was of the essence,
But the inevitable came.
The doctor called the time of death
As the nurse filled out her name.

The team did all they knew to do,
But they couldn't change her fate.
At eighty-six, she breathed her last.
And her body lay in wait.

One by one the team walked out,
And I alone remained
To finish the last details
And disconnect my EKG machine.

As I walked across that empty room,
I clearly heard God say,
"She'll spend eternity separated from Me,
"If you don't stop and pray."

"What can I do? She's dead, Lord!"
But He didn't say a word.
I knew what I was asked to do;
To PRAY is what I heard.

So I walked over to the table,
Her body cold as ice.
I laid my hands, commanding life
In the name of Jesus Christ.

I looked up at the monitor
As the graph began to spike.
Her heart had started beating.
I could hardly believe my eyes.

I ran out to the hallway,
And I called the team back in.
"Her heart has a rhythm!"
And they called her next of kin.

They took her to intensive care,
Not knowing what transpired.
Jesus brought her back to life;
Her love was His desire.

I never saw that kind of LOVE,
To bring her back to life,
To give her one last chance at LOVE,
To choose to be HIS wife.

Two weeks later, she was discharged.
When I took her last EKG,
She took my hand and prayed a prayer,
and BECAME MY FAMILY!

Inspired by God's amazing love,
Faun Collett

Raising Lazarus from the Dead

When I reflect on that experience in the emergency room, I am reminded of Jesus' *heavenly power* when He raised Lazarus from the dead. He shows us the almighty power that God possesses, and we can see that our heavenly Father, the Son, and the Holy Spirit are in control. We need to be aware of the presence of our living God. In the book of John, the evangelist wrote, "Then Jesus, again groaning in Himself, came to the tomb. It was a cave, and a stone lay against it. Jesus said, 'Take away the stone.' Martha, the sister of him who was dead, said to Him, 'Lord, by this time there is a stench, for he has been dead four days.' Jesus said to her, 'Did I not say to you that if you would believe you would see the glory of God?' Then they took away the stone from the place where the dead man was lying. And Jesus lifted up His eyes and said, 'Father, I thank You that You have heard Me. And I know that You always hear Me, but because of the people who are standing by I said this, that they may believe that You sent Me.' Now when He had said these things, He cried with a loud voice, 'Lazarus, come forth!' And he who had died came out bound hand and foot with graveclothes, and his face was wrapped with a cloth. Jesus said to them 'Loose him, and let him go'" (John 11:38–44).

I encourage you to seek Him to know Him personally, so you, too, can become part of God's family—and even raise the dead! We must remember there are more kinds of death than physical. For example, there are family divisions, spiritual separation from God, dying relationships, and disappointments that are devastating in life.

Listening for the Whispers

In the book of John, Jesus said, "My sheep hear My voice, and I know them, and they follow Me. And I give them eternal life, and they shall never perish; neither shall anyone snatch them out of My hand" (John 10:27–28). He's always talking to us, but we don't always listen. Many years ago, I was walking down a road in Fairfield Bay, Arkansas, when God's voice **whispered** into my spirit. I was visiting my parents at their vacation home, and I decided to take a walk to pray and spend time with Jesus. As I was praying, the Lord spoke to my spirit and told me to go the third house on the right and tell the people there that He had sent me.

I stopped for a moment and thought, *That's not God. I must be hearing things!* I continued to walk, and again, God spoke. I had a choice: to look like a fool and knock on that door, or to ignore the voice of God! Missing God was just not an option as far as I was concerned, so I went over and knocked on that door. A woman opened the door, and I could see she had been crying. I told her that I was there visiting my parents, walking down the road, and praying, when God told me to knock on her door and tell her He had sent me to her! She invited me in and told me her daughter had just been in a terrible car accident. Every bone in her body was broken, and they didn't expect her to live, but if she did, she had so much brain damage that she would be nothing more than a vegetable. She had been crying out to God to please send someone to pray with her and agree with her for her daughter's healing. We got down on our knees on her living room floor and prayed. To make a long story short, although it didn't happen instantly, her daughter was eventually totally healed, and she went back to college, later graduating with honors!

Often, I am reminded of this precious time with this mother and my prayerful intercession for her daughter. The joy I received by listening and submitting to God's voice has filled my heart and warmed my soul with only a love that God can provide. When God whispers to your heart, rejoice in His presence and be willing to abide with Him.

A Prophetic Word as God Whispered to Me

So many of My children have cried out in despair and emptiness, wondering where I am and feeling disconnected, yet I am omnipresent! So many of those whom I have chosen have fallen into feelings of abandonment, yet I have said that I would never leave or forsake My own!

What distracts and produces LACK,
What makes you think I'm holding back?
Don't you know I'm always there?
I ALWAYS hear the whispered prayer (James 4:1).

Come run into My presence now.
Release your fears; I'll show you how.
Unspeakable joy awaits with love,
Alone with all I've stored above.

Just come and wait! Tarry with Me now.
You're in My plans! Rejoice and smile…
Let Me pour My life in you
To overcome; I'll bring you through.

What's the secret to My best?
Hang out with Me, and you'll be blessed.
Labor to enter into rest,
Labor to enter My Rest.

by Faun Collett

God desires a closeness with us, and it is up to us to seek His presence so we can build that everlasting relationship with our heavenly Father. I implore you today to seek God in your earthly life and listen for the *soft whispers* that God will place on your heart.

Prayer

Dear heavenly Father, Your greatest gift was freely given to those who choose to receive. Your greatest gift was Jesus, and He came for those who would believe and receive. The value of the greatest gift can never be assessed, for there is nothing to compare when God gives His very best. I marvel at the mantel You have sanctified for man to carry in this priceless gift of Your redemption plan. Love is the essence of who You are and who You are in me. The mystery of the ages is Christ in us, the hope of glory. The greatest commandment and commission is to take this gift of love and saturate this sin-stained world with healing from above. So, what is love? I ask myself. And I find out what love is not: It is never boastful, it does not take wrongs suffered, nor harbor evil. It won't hold unforgiveness, bitterness, and strife. It will not break covenant with husband or with wife. This I know about His love: It will never cease, it overcomes a multitude of sins and brings abiding peace, and this free gift that You have given fills me with a peace like no other. Freely You have given, and freely I receive. Trim my lamp, O sweet Spirit. Lamb of God, Your sheep I will feed. Amen.

Notes

Chapter 8

Faun Haven

Paul wrote, "No, dear brothers, I am still not all I should be, but I am bringing all my energies to bear on this one thing: Forgetting the past and looking forward to what lies ahead, I strain to reach the end of the race and receive the prize for which God is calling us up to heaven because of what Christ Jesus did for us" (Philippians 3:13).

Since the beginning of time, human beings have chosen to disobey God and go our own way. We still make this choice today. This results in separation from God. Romans 3:23 says, "For all have sinned and fall short of the glory of God." Sin is choosing to say, do, or think things that are against

God's plan. "The result of unforgiven sin is death. But God's gift is eternal life given by Jesus Christ our Lord." There is only one way to reach God.

Doug and Faun

After I went through my divorce, a great void hovered over me. I felt defeated, abandoned, and lonely. My pity parties were useless and unfruitful, so I again immersed myself in the Bible and cried out to God for help. I realized that many other believers were facing the same sense of despair, and instead of focusing on my losses, I joined a study at church to begin the healing process and reach out to similar hurting, broken, and downhearted siblings in Christ. Needless to say, you can never outgive God, and lifelong friendships were built at this time. During one of our group events, I met my husband, Doug, and without a clue, new beginnings were on my doorstep. It was a match made in heaven, and our thirty-one-year journey has been one of love, adventure, ministry, and bliss (other than a few kinks here and there). It's true that iron sharpens iron, and after all these years, we have turned out to be a pretty sharp couple, still deeply in love with each other and our Lord Jesus. The poem below is a tribute to God for the gift of my husband, Doug.

A New Beginning

A new beginning beckons, stirring dormant seeds to waken.
A songbird calls my heart to rise from winter hibernation,
And all the silence nature held with breath so icy still
Must once again retreat the sound,
NEW YEAR, NEW LIFE, NEW WILL!

And eager now to quench the thirst
Such slumber tends to bring,
My heart is filled with spring-fed joy
Your lyrics bade me sing.

With gentleness you cover me;
With peace your love flows in;
And joyfully I celebrate
What's come alive again.

Inspired by the hummingbird,
While humming dare not rest,
With zeal she draws sweet nectar,
With care secures her nest.

And sweeter nectar honey
Ne'er bloomed to grace my life.
I'm so proud that you're my husband
And so blessed to be your wife.

Seasons laced with sorrow
Camouflaged this legacy.
God saved the best for last, my love,
When He saved you for me.

by Faun Collett

Doug's Story, a tribute to the man who built our dream while honoring God's vision

Doug and I were married in 1990, and one year later I got a call from his employer. He was taken up in a forklift, twenty feet above the concrete floor to complete some work. Unfortunately, the forklift driver forgot to lock the cage. When Doug was hoisted to the top level, Doug signaled the driver to stop. When he did the cage flipped over causing it to cascade twenty feet to what could have been certain death. Just before landing on the cold, hard concrete floor, Doug flipped upside down and squarely bounced off the side of the steel cage. He hit the corner of the cage and his buttocks caught the blunt end of the fall. He landed on the concrete and was later told his back had been broken. Doug's injuries was conveniently hidden from Doug for over two years by Workman's Comp.

Because of the accident, Doug suffered depilating migraines headaches and unbelievable trauma. He would stay downstairs in a dark room with a wet towel over his eyes. He experienced so much pain that he crawled to the bathroom because he could not walk. Eventually, he had to go to a trauma councilor because he experienced dreams and fears of falling from great heights.

We moved seven times that following year and barley survived, but God always came through just in time.

Someone once said to me, "You live from one crisis to another crises." I said you are wrong. We live from one victory to the next because God is on our side and He will never leave or forsake us.

The pain Doug suffered was excruciating and against threats from Workman's Comp he decided to go to a private doctor. The doctor took x-rays and informed us that Doug's back had been broken and was not healing correctly. This new found knowledge prompted Doug to hire an attorney to defend him against the company and Workman's Comp. Through all of this Doug walked out his faith, and so did I. We prayed and pursued God with all our heart. One particular day I told God about a healing service at a church over and hours' drive away from us, and he said he would like to go. A guest speaker, Rodney Brown, from South Africa came to bring a healing word, and we were expectant for God to move in our lives and heal Doug. But when we got to the church, we began to pray for the evening service. We returned home after praise and worship. We decided to go back to the church for the evening worship, even though it was a two-hour round trip.

I was so disappointed for Doug, who was still suffering from severe back pain and a debilitating migraine, but he was determined to go back to church for the evening service. During that service, the worship team began to minister to the Lord and Doug began to pray for the sick for quite some time. At just the perfect time, Mr. Brown went up to the podium and immediately called Doug out by name. He pointed straight at the center mid-section where Doug was seated and said, "You, your Doug. Come up here God's healing your back. Doug was mesmerized. Thinking how does he know about my back? How did he get my name all the while walking his way towards the center aisle? By the time he reached the middle aisle, he stopped and turned to look over to me, signaling that the migraine had left him, and all the pain in his back had vanished. He felt a pop, pop, pop like a vise going up his spine and could go any further. Dropping to his knees with hands in the air and tears flowing down his cheeks, Doug was miraculously healed. There is so much more I could say, but the hand of God was lovingly on my husband, and my husband was giving God all the glory. If that healing had not happened, Doug would have remained physically challenged and our dreams would never become a reality. But for God's sake, Doug's health was restored, renewed, and healed. Because of this miracle from God, Doug labored to enhance the vision and build our dream while focusing on serving God.

After his healing, Doug had to face the workman's comp doctor, and he knew the consequences would affect his ruling for compensation from his back injurers. He felt foolish going to that meeting, but he carried his back brace into their office and told them, "Jesus healed my back." He knew there would be a price to pay for such a disclosure, and he sure didn't know it would just about finish us financially. We had waited years without an income, and we had absolutely nothing to fall back on to sustain us economically. When we went to the attorney to settle the workman's comp case, we didn't even get enough money to pay Doug's medical bills, but that did not deter Doug's faith in God. He said he would rather err on the side of Jesus, and he would rather go with God than man. That is the kind of man Doug is. He is a drummer who walks to a different beat. He has integrity, and he is the muscle behind everything we ever did. He would be digging ditches and thinking about *The Fiddler on the Roof*, where the man cried out to God, "Can You just make it a little bit easier?"

What Doug had to do was backbreaking, but he never missed a beat. He worked full-time and still cleared and settled the land that we had bought. He was a jack-of-all trades and a man of most. He never ceased to amaze me; he never quit, never slowed down, and stayed steadfast with his communication with our heavenly Father as he worked the land. He shared with me that he prayed, talking to God all day when he was at work. He had a relationship with the Father that was meaningful, and his relationship with me was anchored in Christ. A man who loves God will know how to love a woman, and Doug brought a whole new meaning to our love.

As a young teenager, he daydreamed of having a place in the woods at the end of the road, with a few golden retrievers by his side. Years later, he had a flashback of his dreams and realized that God had honored the desires of his heart. When our home was completed, Doug told the Lord, "You have given us this home and land. It is a blessing straight from Your hand, and the least we can do is open this place as a home-away-from-home for those who need a respite, and a place to meet and get to know the One who loves the most." Thus, Faun Haven was birthed from the tenderhearted man after God's own heart. It was God's gift of hospitality and the love of God that allowed us to share our bounty. Together we embraced the call, and we built a safe haven for over 350 young people who needed hope, future, and a destiny on their horizon with a God who would never leave them nor forsake them.

Dear Holy Abba Father

You're a wonder to behold, and in all Your creation,
Your endless story is told.
Your majesty, Your tapestry, and Your creative flair
Floods my heart with gratitude and
fills my mouth with prayer.
How can it be? Your majesty as Lord of lords and King of kings,
That I have been adopted into this place of royal dreams,
That I can call You Abba with praise and thanksgiving?
My very own daddy, my Abba, Your idea, Your song,
I can't wrap my mind around how You called me to belong.
I was so unworthy then, and I am unworthy still,
But you placed Your seal upon me by Your covenant ad will.
And all the sin that weighed me down,
You cleansed me with holy blood,
O Lamb of God, Anointed One, by Your redeeming flood.
Sealed by Your Holy Spirit dear Abba Father
You have truly set me free
And I am overwhelmed where You have seated me.
To rule and reign forever, Abba Father, throughout eternity.
Ephesians 2:6.

by Faun Collett

Before Doug and I met, we had both been married to unfaithful partners, and we each went through painful breakups, devastations, and financial disasters. Between the two of us, we had five angry and broken teenagers, who, through no fault of their own, had to face a broken home, and we all had to try to pick up the pieces of heartbreak and insecurity. On top of all this, we faced physical devastation when Doug fell twenty feet onto concrete at work, and he lost his job and his income. We were placed into a temporary situation in which we could not support ourselves, take care of our children, or maintain a home.

What we could and did do was cry out to God and pray together for the miracles that we needed to come by His hand. We yielded ourselves to God's direction and remained supportive of each other as we worked together, undivided, as a team. The miracles did, indeed, come, God's hand was definitely upon us, and His blessings were the result. We have been so happy together, serving God and reaching for the goal of developing and growing the vision placed in our heart for homeless youth.

God Will Pave the Way

At times in our marriage, Doug and I were caught off guard, utterly helpless, broke, and living in less-than-favorable conditions, but we knew that God would never leave or forsake us and that "this, too, would pass." The important thing was to lean on God and always acknowledge Him; He would guide us on a pathway that would ultimately glorify Him. It is human nature for us to try to solve our own problems and think it is our responsibility to do so. But if we only had faith and a prayerful encounter with God, everything in life would be less traumatic for us. Heartache and pain are a part of life, and disappointment and loss are inevitable. Tears may fill our eyes and pain may invade our hearts, but as the following poem says, He will collect every teardrop, and the healing will begin.

All Our Tears

Tears are a river fed from the streams
Of nobles, paupers, commoners, and kings.
They break all the barriers common to man.
Tears is a language that God understands.

They are never unnoticed or ignored from above,
Whether emerging in pain or erupting from love.
Though they cry out from the heart, praying deep from within,
Our sweet Father saves them, and the healings begin.

He collects every teardrop so His Kingdom can see
How He paid for each one throughout all eternity.
Where there were tears, they were all wiped away.
Our Father has bottled them for some glad day.

Inspired by a Faithful God,
Faun Collettt

In Psalm 56:8–9, the psalmist prayed: "You number my wanderings; put my tears into Your bottle; are they not in Your book? When I cry out to You, then my enemies will turn back; this I know, because God is for me." God knows the heartaches and pains we face in this earthly life. We were not created to go through life alone. I encourage you to trust in our heavenly Father and seek strength through His mercy and grace.

In 1991, Doug and I faced an extremely difficult time, and if it hadn't been for the obedience of several young men who heard the voice of God, we would have been blindsided by the circumstances we faced. In the first prophecy, the young man saw us in the backseat of a car. We weren't driving ;we were just along for the ride. He told us that a literal move was coming—we ended up moving seven times—but God wanted us to know the moving would eventually stop and we would be where God wanted us to be. In the second prophecy, God shared that He was taking us to a new church and that we were to submit ourselves to the pastor there and he would teach us about how to succeed in business.

Shortly after that, Doug fell over twenty feet while at work, and he ultimately lost his job—and our income. We lost our kennel in a flood and had nowhere to go with our dogs or ourselves. We got down on our knees and prayed together, then we got in the car and Doug drove toward

Warrenton from St. Peters. As we passed a church on the highway, I looked up and saw a sign high on the hill that said, "Jesus Is Alive"! Immediately God spoke to me and said that was the church to which He was calling us. We exited Highway 70, turning south on Highway 47, and as we passed Cannonball, God spoke to me and told me to turn down a certain road. Doug turned around, and we drove to the end of that dead-end road. A man dressed in bib overalls was standing by his mailbox, and I knew I was supposed to talk to him. I got out of the car, walked over, and engaged in conversation with him. I asked if he knew of any property for sale in the area but he did not. I then asked him if he owned the land where we were, and if he would consider selling *five acres* because we wanted to train dogs for the handicapped and we needed a place to live.

He laughed and said that every year scores of people come down the road to ask the same thing, but he and his wife had twenty-seven acres and had lived there for twenty-seven years. They were content just the way they were. I gave him my card and told him to call me if he changed his mind—and the rest is history. The next day he called and said his wife wanted to move to Florida to be with their grandchildren. He offered to sell fifteen acres to us. The owner financed the land, and Faun Haven was born. This, too, was a *miracle* from God so that His prophecy could be fulfilled and His work would be completed at Faun Haven.

This was definitely a miracle, but it didn't stop there. Doug and I needed to set up a temporary dwelling for our dogs and haul water over to them every day, so I went to our neighbors and asked if we could lease water from them. The lady said, "Honey, I'm an intercessor. Do you know what that is?" I said, "Yes—because I, too, am an intercessor!" She told us that God had just spoken to her and said Doug and I were to live in her home for one year rent-free before we moved onto our own land. She said we could build a kennel in her backyard until we were able to move.

When Doug went over to talk with her, she shook her finger at him and said, "Listen here, young man. I know the voice of God, and I know what He told me. You're to live here rent-free for one year and raise your dogs on this land until you move onto your own land—and I won't take no for an answer!" She drew up a contract and had it notarized at her bank, and so Doug and I had a home and a new beginning. Shortly after that, I went to a shoe store and met *Nedra* and *Earnie*, who invited me to my first visit at *Faith Christian Family Church*. Just like that, we had a new church home.

God's Work Is Never Easy

In 1995, Doug and I began the Academy of Missouri Educational Network of Graduate Dogs, Inc.; we also worked a foster program and an at-risk program as well as a step down and recovery program later down the road. It has never been easy, and every step of the way, we had to labor hard and adjust over and over again as we discovered that God's timing and ways are higher and better than ours. We knew that to whom much is given, much is required, and that it is our responsibility to oversee and be wise stewards over His affairs.

While we were building the kennel facilities, Doug worked (after his back was broken) all the overtime he could get, doing hard labor on diesel engines at the railyards in East St. Louis. He drove a total more than three to four hours a day, depending on the traffic, then come home dog-tired and go to work building the house and kennels, putting in landscaping, and tending to anything else that needed his attention. After his day's work was done, he would sleep a few hours, then start all over. During that time, I functioned as the general contractor for the house, working out every detail, purchasing all the supplies, working with the banks, and hiring and managing the subcontractors. I, too, was busy with other goals, attending the International School for Ministry, networking, and eventually earning my associate's degree from Vision University. After that, I served two years in the bridge program working with Pastor Terry on church government. Our lives were busy beyond compare, but they were blessed as well. God gave us the strength to accomplish much in life, and we sought to serve Him as we reached out to others so they, too, could know the love that only God can provide.

As the president of Faun Haven Kennels, Inc., and the president of the Academy of Missouri Educational Network of Graduate Dogs, Inc., I was often up until three or four in the morning, handling my administrative responsibilities as well as charting dogs, sales, taxes, etc. Daily, we were challenged with bodies that were wasting away, but inwardly we were growing in maturity and sensitivity to the Lord. At this time in our journey with God, we began to take in individuals who were destitute, lost, and without hope. Our goal was to be an instrument of the Lord by bringing individuals into our home. Our hope was to introduce them to our heavenly Father and guide them into their own walk with God.

Because of our desire to help others, we needed a set of rules that not only worked for us, but also for everyone whose presence graced our home. We made lifelong relationships with those in need and were shown respect in return. Most importantly, we saw lives changed and God's family increase in number. What a blessing this time was in our lives!

A God-Centered Declaration

We now had our property, our kennels, our home, our resources, and our ministry, and until God passes this privilege on to someone else, we have the final word. As Pastor Terry has often told his staff, anyone who tries to devalue, undermine, or in general cause dissension, spread division, or disrespect our authority will be dealt with immediately. We realize that those tactics are directly related to Satan's plans to destroy what God has begun, and that cannot happen here.

We told those who stayed with us that if they had a problem, they should come to us, and we would listen, pray, and make the final decision concerning the matter. They were grown individuals, there by their own choice, and it was their responsibility to keep the peace and go through the right channels to resolve issues, rather than gossiping among themselves like a bunch of idle busybodies. If they couldn't say anything good, they should say nothing at all!

I also made it crystal-clear that they were not our responsibility; they were our colaborers in a work that God had begun. They were not there for a vacation, nor was our home a place where they would bide their time until something better came along. No, they were there by divine appointment and by their own choice. No one was holding them there against their will, and as long as they were there, they were expected to honor God, respect those in authority, and as much as it was possible, live in peace with each other.

No matter where they were in their walk with God, as long as they resided on our premises, they were to respect certain guidelines, and our policy was ZERO TOLERANCE.

1. *REFRAIN FROM IMMORAL BEHAVIORS and FOUL TALK.*

2. *REFRAIN FROM DRUG USE OR ABUSE OF CHEMICALS.*

3. *REFRAIN FROM SMOKING IN THE HOME or THE KENNEL (other than in designated areas outside).*

4. *Be responsible with the Chart of Kitchen Duty, and only do your laundry on appointed days and before nighttime. Showers should be taken during the morning or early evening before 7 p.m. (Doug and I liked to take our baths at night, and we wanted to have hot water to do so.)*

5. *When you work outside the home, you will be expected to pay $28 a day for your part if you can't put in your four hours here. The only exception to this rule would be if you banked your hours to make them up during weekends, as long as you have approval from Doug or myself ahead of time.*

6. *If you spend any nights elsewhere or have other plans, they must be brought to our attention at least forty-eight hours ahead of time and you must you're your work hours.*

7. *You are expected to follow the guidelines of the chart on the garage door for keeping your living quarters clean, vacuumed, and dusted, and the bathroom, shower, and toilet cleaned daily.*

8. *Attending church on Sundays (or Saturday nights) has always been an expectation.*

9. *Attending meetings for recovery is also encouraged.*

10. *If you have any needs for toiletries, food items, etc., please make a list and put it on the fridge.*

11. *Make it your job daily to find a job.*

12. *If you need prayer, please write down your request, and we will lift you up.*

May God richly bless your stay here! Our goal is to help you through this transitional time and see you working, self-sufficient (with Christ's help), and living out your own dreams by following the path God has for you. However, until you reach that goal, you are expected to work a program of recovery, read God's Word, worship Him, and develop a relationship with Jesus that will carry you on to victorious living.

If Doug and I feel you are not living in a way that honors God or those around you, we will not hesitate to request that you leave. Your security is not in us, but in the King of kings. We know there is nothing the King won't do for His children, but we also know God will not call His children those who choose to walk in rebellion and disobedience. Jesus said, "If he loves Me, he will keep My word; and My Father will love him, and We will come to him and make Our home with him" (John 14:23). He also said, "If anyone desires to come after Me, let him deny himself, and take up his cross daily, and follow Me" (Luke 9:23), and God tells us to "[cast] all your care upon Him, for He cares for you" (1 Peter 5:7). Jesus held nothing back, not even His own death, so that you could live by dying to self and breathing in the life He purchased for you. You wanted to make the trade: all of your unrighteousness for all of His righteousness. He didn't force anything on you. You have chosen life and made Him Lord! He paid a dear price of great worth for you because of His great love toward you. Now live as if your life is no longer yours, but His. He'll do a better job with it, and you'll reap eternal rewards, but you must learn how to surrender all. Jesus told us to seek first the Kingdom of God and His righteousness, and everything else would be added to us. You'll never find a better deal than that. Amen!

A Full-Circle Program

Doug and I believe we were brought together by divine providence and God's purpose for our lives. Although we had to work through many challenges and trials, our track record has proven to be rock-solid and trustworthy. During our adventures together, we have weathered caring for many teenagers, foster children, and homeless, abused, and abandoned individuals. We helped each of them through many storms in their lives. Along with a commitment to shelter, guide, protect, and mentor these young people, we used our unique talents—and our faithful dogs—to build an organization that Doug calls a *Full-Circle Program*. Along with experiential education, animal therapy, and a family concept, over two hundred young people have graced our doorstep and have benefited from the training and bonding exercises we have shared with our gentle, faithful canines. They have gleaned great leadership skills through these caring, nurturing behaviors.

By practicing praise, reward, and positive reinforcement, and by walking away when angry, only to return with a calm, assertive attitude, our patience has paid off. These diversion tactics help ensure patience and self-control when they begin to parent their own future children themselves. The work ethic they develop helps to equip them for their future jobs and sensitizes them to the teamwork needed to succeed in the workplace. For several years, Doug and I taught life skills in a new pilot program for the state of Missouri, taking institutionalized youth and integrating them into neighborhoods through rental homes. This experience, along with their training, helped equip them for the *Ready, Set, Fly* initiative contracted by the state to teach foster parents how to help transition youth who were aging out of state care. The transitional skills taught by Doug and me included other areas such as guidance, financial peace through learning money management, continuing education while developing character, trust, and respect for their fellow man, and focusing on their dreams and what it takes to achieve them. During this time, we found ourselves in constant prayer for these precious souls, and God continually *whispered* His peace into our lives.

During the next stage of our development, I applied and was approved for a nonprofit organization called the Academy of Missouri Educational Network of Graduate Dogs, Inc., (AMEN), sometimes called Amendogs. Within this organizational vision, the bigger picture says it best. Doug had been teaching leadership using the natural training methods of caring and providing for the dogs as their alpha would do. He and I both worked with at-risk youth, abused girls, and A+ honor students who came to help mentor those who struggled during the pilot program for the school district. The alternative students went from 30 percent to 80 percent grade point averages. On one particular day, an alternative student requested permission to work at the kennels unaccompanied. Permission was granted, and later this hardworking young man came back with his hands bleeding. He had been too "macho" to wear gloves. He asked us a simple request, to view the surprise he had worked so hard on; he had built an exercise play yard for the dogs' free time. Because we lived on a ridge, the ground was hard and rocky. This young man had had to dig postholes and stretch the fence by himself—quite a feat for a fourteen-year-old boy! We were so impressed by his thoughtfulness and hard work that I asked him to document what he had accomplished in his student folder. His reaction was heartrending. He said, *"We ain't nothing but worms; nobody cares what we think, and I don't need to document nothin'."* I immediately responded with conviction: "You are not a worm! You may not fit behind a desk like other students. It is not your gift. Look what you just did for us and for the dogs. You are a treasure beyond measure, and your gift will make room for you. I never want to hear you say that you are nothing but a worm again!" That night I prayed, "Lord, how can I show educators what is happening here?" God woke me up at 2:30 a.m. with the following poem. This poem came from the inspiration of the young people's working vision and from the heart of the One who brought them together "for such a time as this." The bigger picture says it all:

The Bigger Picture

One day a worm was murmuring as he
burrowed through the soil.
How very hard his lot has been to press and push and toil.
The ground's so hard, with clumps of clay
that feel like moving gravel.
The path of such a lowly worm's not an easy road to travel.

A glorious wildflower stands alone amidst the forest edge.
Full-bloomed with beauty unsurpassed, this pretty flower said,
"What's wrong with me? I know I'm pretty;
not only that, I'm smart.
"Why was I placed out here alone to die of a broken heart?"

"I have so much to offer; my dreams surpass this place.
"Rare medicine flows through my veins
that could help the human race.
"Yet it seems I am forsaken; birds and bees and butterfly
"Sucking the life right out of me, while I wither here and die."

As the little flower wilted, a seed dropped with her fears.
Encasing all within her heart, the "promise" bathed in tears.
One night a child was pondering the mystery of the stars:
Could there be life on planets like Jupiter and Mars?

The child grew daily, seeking how to quench
his thirst for knowledge,
And it wasn't long before this child was heading off for college.
An expedition followed, and not knowing what he'd need.
He found himself on the forest floor, discovering a seed.

This seed must be protected and have every chance to grow,
For only when it comes to life will we have the chance to know
What promises it carries, the incubated dreams,
So, he took some soil and samples for the laboratory teams.

And they, in turn, had found a worm
who worked the soil so smooth.
They planned to use this rich worm's bed
for the special seeds they'd use.
Can you see the paradox, my friend,
can you guess the final phase?
How a lowly worm and a lonely flower left a legacy of praise!

For when their purpose was fulfilled,
and their fate had stood the test,
New medicine was mass-produced,
bringing healing, peace, and rest.
And let us not forget that child who makes
the world much richer,
When he's given room and open doors,
to explore the bigger picture!

The worms may seem to be at risk, the flowers mirror girls,
Abused and used, both unaware that they're priceless,
treasured pearls.
In case you've overlooked the point or failed
to see the hidden part,
Let's go back to the beginning to the worm and flower's heart.

by Faun Collett

Our youth are like delicate flowers. They must be cared for, cultivated, and loved so they can thrive and grow in God's grace. This poem actually had nothing to do with dogs, but it had everything to do with the beautiful giftings God has equipped His creation with—all for His glory. We must remember that our youth have more difficult challenges in life than we did when we were young. Young people who have been in the foster or correctional systems have it even tougher. Making the transition from dependency to independence can be trying for any of us. It's especially hard for those who have been dumped without skills or direction into the mainstream. But time, training, and maturity can play a big part in salvaging their lives and ensuring their success. Remember you, too, can make a difference in a person's life; when God gives you the opportunity to share His message with them or simply say a prayer for them, listen to His whispering voice and fulfill the purpose God has for you.

Our mission to help others was not always a tranquil venture, but God was with us every step of the way. We built Faun Haven Board and Breed, as well as a nonprofit organization called the Academy of Missouri Educational Network of Graduate Dogs, Inc. Over time we took in over 350 people from all walks of life, mostly youth, and we have worked a life skills program with animal therapy for them. The journey has been amazing and rewarding. Most of all, we have been instrumental in leading many to Jesus and watching *Him* take it from there. Doug has called it a Full-Circle Program, and although we have downsized and made some adjustments, we continue to work with those whom God brought our way. Our mission was God-centered, and we were blessed to serve the Lord. Many people have graced our home with their presence, and we helped them find their hope, future, and destiny in Him.

Louie Tells His Story: An Inspirational Message:

Louie

Mom and Dad divorced when I was seven years old. They reconciled and then split up again! That was probably harder than the first time because the fighting and strife seemed to be worse. I was about eleven (in the fifth grade), and I felt sad, but I still had love from Mom, Dad, and my grandparents and uncles. Through the years, because of Dad being gone, the lack of money in the home took its toll on everyone. We really learned how to stretch a dollar. At the age of twelve, I was the "man of the house," and I probably had to grow up faster than I normally would have. God sheltered me throughout my childhood, but because of the divorce, I had to leave my private school and friends to go to a public school. I experienced a lot of new emotions, and I wanted to fit in. I became popular with the girls.

In junior high, I began to experiment with drugs and then alcohol. By the time I graduated from high school, I was drinking every night. I loved to party, and I made money selling and using drugs. It began to take a toll on me.

I worked hard and was highly respected in the carpet industry until my habits put a strain on my overall performance.

I had several lasting relationships that went on for three or four years, but by the time I was thirty, I just hadn't connected with anyone. So, from that time until I was in my mid-forties, drugs and alcohol filled the voids in my life. I hung out with the wrong people, and the Bible says, "Bad company corrupts good morals" (1 Corinthians 15:33 AMP).

I have always had a gift to reach out to people and help them, but having a servant's heart when you're not serving God will backfire.

Soon, I developed a no-care attitude about authority, and after several DWIs, I began driving without a license, and I went back and forth on that roller coaster for some time. Eventually the law caught up with me, and I spent the greater part of a year in jail. Unable to make my house payments, I made a quick sale of my house and lost a huge amount of money, as well as literally all of my possessions other than a few items of clothing.

My relationship with my father was strained to the point that he would have nothing to do with me. We had always been close, so this affected me deeply, and I began to isolate myself.

Eventually I was back in jail, and at that time, I wasn't completely yielded to God. I still went to church every week, and I was always trying to get my mom and sisters to minister to guys who were down and out and needed God's help. One was led to a personal relationship with the Lord as a result of those visits! I wanted to help them recover, even though I still had my own issues to deal with.

After I was released from jail, I had nowhere to live. I went to stay with my mom and stepfather for about nine months, and I was basically dormant and reclusive, spending a great amount of time in my room reading but really not doing much of anything else. I regularly attended church with my mom and stepfather, and I'd try to help with projects here and there, but my family felt I wasn't moving forward and that I needed a change.

They called friends from their church who had a ministry helping people get on their feet again; my parents asked me to pack up my small bag of belongings, and the next thing I knew, I had moved to Faun Haven. Doug and Faun are the ministry founders and leaders of Faun Haven as well as a nonprofit organization called AMEN Dogs, with a vision to help others work with dogs, learn to train them, and hopefully in the future, place them as service and support dogs for the disabled.

At Faun Haven Kennel, I started on my journey with the Bible, and that is when a true transformation started to take place in my life. I began to work there in exchange for my room and board. Doug and Faun opened their home to me, as well as took me to church—the same one my family attended. When I started reading the Bible, I received healing in my heart. You could say the light was turned up and I saw the Truth as never before. The Scripture says, "Your word is a lamp to my feet and a light to my path" (Psalm 119:105). I am so thankful that the Light of Christ is in me, empowering me to be more than I ever could have ben in the natural realm.

Eventually, I took an interest in some leadership courses that had a Christian foundation, and I began to realize that being a leader started with those Christian principles. As time went on, I listened to Christian CDs and read the Bible every chance I got. I began to understand my love language (what naturally motivated me and what I was learning to share), and I began developing the natural gifts that God had given me, even as a child, including the gift of helps, as defined in book of Corinthians. I made myself available to the church to help clean, empty trash, lay carpet, repair things, and set up for special events; basically I just plugged in to help wherever I could. I learned the value of building relationships with other believers, and I was able to take on a part-time job with a sign company and then book a few carpet jobs here and there.

I've been at Faun Haven for almost five and a half years, and I have had the opportunity to meet many others who have shared my living quarters. Now I have a part in helping others find their place in God's plan for their life, not just by training them in animal care, but by giving them encouragement. God has a hope, a future, and a destiny for them, as well. I walk alongside them to help them discover and develop their God-given gifts, and then I help them to return to a normal, productive life.

Eventually, I began serving in the bus ministry at Faith Christian Family Church (FCFC) in 2010. FCFC has a ministry to reach out to those in the community who otherwise wouldn't be able to attend church. During my involvement in the bus ministry, I was able to find a source to provide Bibles for every child who rode the bus, and I have been there to encourage them to read and memorize Scripture, as well as share with them how to find the Scriptures they want to read.

I have always loved God, but I did not realize I could have a rich and meaningful relationship with Him instead of just religion. I began to see the value of giving back to God one-tenth of my first and my best income, and I discovered that you cannot outgive God!

My earthly father's heart is softening toward me now as he truly sees the transformation in my life. I have begun the process of restoring our relationship.

God has definitely blessed my life in more ways than I have time to tell, but one of the greatest blessings has been to come all this way to testify of His goodness to you. At the same time, I have been blessed to receive a healing touch from the people that I couldn't find back home. God is so good, and His mercy is brand-new every morning. Serving Him is just the beginning of new beginnings for me—and a lifetime of bringing honor and glory to Him!

As I reflect on Louie's struggles, accomplishments, and walk with God, I am reminded that everyone faces issues beyond their control, especially when circumstances seem to dictate bleak, down-and-out times that call for time alone with God. Ultimately, that is when we need to regroup, renew, and refresh ourselves and draw closer to our heavenly Father. It took Louie some time to fulfill his destiny, and he now has a testimony to share with others who might be going through situations that seem bleak and hopeless. Louie was a blessing in our lives, and God has used him to reach others who need someone just like Louie. Today, he is a missionary in the Philippines and serving God in an unbelievable ministry. He is a gift from God, and we are so blessed that God brought him into our lives. When I think of Louie, I think of all the other lost and struggling souls who crossed our paths.

Child of Hope

Dear child, you're not defeated
If you don't buy into the lie!
It's the devil's greatest weapon,
To deceive you till you die.

He is the father of the carnal mind,
But he is not a caring dad,
For his purpose is his vengeance,
And that's all he's ever had.

Like seed bears its likeness,
Bad seed distorts the plant.
To learn to recognize bad seed,
You must throw out "I can't"!

For you can do all things, dear child,
Through Jesus Christ, your Lord.
The lie is that it costs too much,
And that living right is hard.

But deep inside your spirit,
You know what's brought you pain

And stolen much of love and youth
And weighed you down with blame.

Don't buy it, child, don't buy it.
Lies hold the greatest price.
Sin cannot bring you comfort
Without rolling loaded dice.

The truth is, there are riches
That money cannot buy,
But you're an heir of fortunes,
Blessings, treasures piled so high.

So high, no one can steal them
For they are locked up in your soul.
Jesus has the combination
To enrich and make you whole.

Don't give the Gift away, dear one,
Don't covet deadly seed.
Trust Jesus, child, with all your heart.
He'll give you all you need.

Inspired by a need for the hurting,
Faun Collett

God so desperately wants to comfort and save struggling souls who have been influenced by the devil's work. I encourage you to reach out to the weak and spiritually afflicted whom you meet. Show them God's love, introduce them to the Healer of all their afflictions, and invite them to know God on a personal basis.

Spiritual Guidance for MISSY MAE

Faun and Doug,

I want to thank you both from the bottom of my heart for what you both have done for me. Today was the most unforgettable day I have ever experienced in all my life. I thank God for each of you, because if it wasn't for the both of you, I wouldn't be closer to God, and I wouldn't have known what it felt like to have Christian friends or a Christian home.

I am blessed to have all I have. I know I get stressed out sometimes and lose my cool. But both of you help to keep me rational and loving the life God gave me. I sincerely believe God has a plan for me and that I am where I am supposed to be. Even though life gets hard and I feel like I want to give up and throw in the towel every now and then, I remember everything each of you taught me: "That I should cast all my cares upon the Lord, for he careth for me" (1 Peter 5:7), and that "I have the mind of Christ" (1 Corinthians

2:16; Philippians 2:5). "May the God of hope fill you with all joy and peace as you trust in him, so that you may overflow with hope by the power of the Holy Spirit" (Romans 15:13 NIV). If it weren't for my God, I would have given up a long time ago and let this world devour me.

But by the grace of God, I am still here and fighting the good fight of faith! So, I will end this thank-you letter with a sincere thank-you! I love you both so very much! Thank you, guys, for being my spiritual guides!

Sincerely, Missy Mae

God has a purpose for each of us, and He has included you in that purpose, as well. We are given opportunities to minister to others and lead people to Christ. This purpose is a blessing from God, and when He gives you the opportunity to introduce others to Him, embrace it with love and serve Him with all your heart. Listen for His *whispers*, for He will guide you as you go.

When Doug and I decided to become foster parents, we did not come to the decision without great prayer. We began to foster small children, but later we were presented with the challenge of rebellious, angry, and defiant teens. We knew that no one else wanted them, but they were God's treasures and He would give us the patience and skill to help these young, lost, and abandoned souls. They came from broken homes, where dysfunctional parents were unable to meet their children's basic needs. One day we were contacted by Family Services about three teenage siblings. Their father was in prison and missing from the family unit, and their mother had waxed cold to the three precious teens who would become our foster children. I remember them well, because they had such a desire to stay together as a family. They told us that the night before they came to us they had stood and prayed all night for God to send them to a home where they could remain together. This was a *miracle* because these three young, precious souls had not even been exposed to the love of God, yet they possessed enough faith to pray. The following three poems give insight into the lives of these precious, young teens and show that God's grace was in their lives. He wants to cover you with His grace, as well.

Elvis L. Brandon

Elvis L. Brandon walked in our lives when he was just sixteen.
He came with lots of baggage, but he barely owned a thing!
His young life was interrupted because of choices not his own.
Now his sister and little brother were all he had left from home.

Lots of weight was on his shoulders, as the oldest in his clan.
When he really should have been a boy, he had to be a man.
I hear he prayed with urgency that the Father up above
Would bring them to a place that cared, someone to give them love.

I wasn't there to hear that prayer, but I know how Elvis came,
For Doug and I had also prayed God's will in Jesus' name.
Now seventeen and walking tall, Elvis is in our home,
Living with his family, and we're proud of how he's grown.

We know that in a little while, Elvis will need to go,
Not because we send him, but because life will make it so.
When that time comes, Doug and I will pray another prayer:
"Thank You, God, for Elvis, please be with him everywhere!"

You've given us great memories and precious times to share.
The world may never recognize the treasures we've had here.
For many families build their lives and have their fame to sing,
But few have had the privilege of living with ELVIS, THE KING!

by Faun Collett

Jamie Sue Is Sweet Sixteen

Jamie Sue Scates is SWEET sixteen, and anyone can see
That she'll never be as pretty as she is right now to me!
I'm her foster mother, and I wanted her to know
That she's pretty as a picture, and her beauty's sure to grow.

Beauty can be measured, and the world is sometimes cruel.
So many try to send their girls away to beauty school.
But Jamie has a secret, and most can't pass this test.
Her beauty comes from Jesus, and she's
INSIDE/OUT the BEST!

We're so thankful that she came to us, so we could be a part
Of passing on to Jamie, a little of God's heart.
Sometimes a word like "little" might hint at something small,
But a "little" of the heart of God, is more than a word like "ALL."

Her friends might call her midget, and laugh at her tiny frame,
Or tease her when she makes mistakes and often acts insane.
Sometimes she's hard to figure out,
and sometimes she does no wrong.
Just SWEET 16 and teaching us her priceless "JAMIE" song!

My prayer is every birthday that comes to "JAMIE SCATES"
Will be to all around her the "BEST TO CELEBRATE!"
As far as foster parents, as long as we're on earth,
We'll sing each day in some "small" way,
the joy of Jamie's birth!

by Faun Collett

Jonathan Lee

Jonathan Lee was presented to me
when he was fourteen years young.
The baby in his family was now to be our son.
His brother and sister joined him with a pledge to stay together,
And Doug and I began to pray that God
would make things better.

We knew this curly-headed boy was hurting from the start,
And it would take a miracle to heal his breaking heart.
Though Jon was younger than his siblings, we soon came to see
The gifts God placed within him would help to set him free.

There isn't much that Jon can't do when he makes up his mind.
He's not afraid to work with goals and won't leave much behind,
But pieces of the puzzle Jon will need to take him places
Can only fit when Jon discovers the Holy Spirit's spaces.

He's so very young and yet so strong, with the will to overcome.
I pray that Doug and I can pave the way for the race he has to run.
For FAITH is the path before him,
and he needs to find God's light
To guide him and to heal him and
to get him through the night.

Forgiveness is the hiking boots that Jon will need to wear.
The fruit of the Spirit is the fuel to take him everywhere.
The road before him may be rocky and a little thorny,
But Jesus will go with him, and His joy comes in the morning!

by Faun Collett

220

Suggested Scriptures

Psalm 139 is a beautiful psalm I recommend you read when you get some quiet time. It speaks volumes as to how attentive God really is to you.

Hebrews 12:1 tells us to strip off anything that slows us down or holds us back, especially those sins that wrap themselves so tightly around our feet and trip us up. We are tp run with patience the particular race that God has set before us. To sum up what Pastor Terry always taught us, humility is the ability to receive what we will never deserve! We are changed by what we know. The Bible says that we will know the truth (*Jesus*), and the truth will set us free. He whom the Son sets free is free indeed! It's the goodness of God that leads us to changing our hearts and minds. It is not by our power or might, but by God's Spirit that we can change as we give Him permission to invade our space and honor Him.

Faun Haven had the goal to help displaced youth prepare for a positive future, where they could become productive and follow the purpose that God had for their lives. As I reflect on that time in our lives, I am reminded that "God makes a home for the lonely; He leads out the prisoners into prosperity, only the rebellious live in parched lands" (Psalm 68:6 NASB1995). We encouraged them to hold fast to their dreams, and we assured them of God's hope, future, and destiny.

Prayer

Dear heavenly Father,

May every person who reads these words identify with Your calling on their lives. May Your anointing prepare them to discern Your still, gentle whispers and help them to see that You are much more than a religion. As they journey through life, may Your whispers begin to awaken them to the hope, future, and destiny You have for them, and may You prepare them to hear Your call upon their lives. In Jesus' name we pray, amen.

Notes

Notes

Chapter 9

You Need a Camel for the Wilderness

In Isaiah 61:1–3 the prophet said, "The Spirit of the Sovereign LORD is on me, because the LORD has anointed me to proclaim good news to the poor. He has sent me to bind up the brokenhearted, to proclaim freedom for the captives and release from darkness for the prisoners, to proclaim the year of the LORD's favor and the day of vengeance of our God, to comfort all who mourn, and provide for those who grieve in Zion—to bestow on them a crown of beauty instead of ashes, the oil of joy instead of mourning, and a garment of praise instead of a spirit of despair. They will be called oaks of righteousness, a planting of the LORD for the display of his splendor" (NIV).

For many years, God had been equipping Doug and me for His glory, and He *whispered* to me, reaffirming His purpose for our lives. I had gone to Bible school, earned a degree, and even functioned in pastoral leadership positions, and I had been ordained through Faith Christian Fellowship in 2004. Most importantly, I have seen God perform miracles in people's lives, and I have had the opportunity to share the glory of God with many lost and abandoned souls. While I was privileged to see His works and how His presence changes people's lives, I was being equipped for my final mission on earth: to serve the spiritual needs of the lost and disheartened souls at the House of Transfiguration, the ultimate calling given to me by God.

My equipping and preparation for the work of God has been ongoing for decades. I remember a time when I was invited to speak to a group of women entrepreneurs who were meeting at a Hampton Inn. I had prepared a fantastic message on holding fast to your dreams, and I was excited about the opportunity to share my testimony of God opening doors for my husband and me to fulfill the dream He had placed in our hearts. But I got into my car, God spoke to me. He said, *"The title of your message is 'For Such a Time as This'."* I immediately responded, "No, it's not. the title of my message is 'Hold Fast to Your Dreams'." Of course, God's not into arguing, so as I was driving, He gave me a song, and I worshiped Him with that song while I drove. It was out of the book of Revelation:

> *I have seen the work that you have done. I have seen your joy and compassion, but this one thing I have and am not pleased, you have left your first love. Return, return, return to your first love. Return, return, return to your first love.*

I sang that over and over, and then God spoke again: *"The title of your message is 'For Such a Time as This'!"* By the time I got to the parking lot of the Hampton Inn, I'd decided to look up in my Bible the phrase "for such a time as this." I didn't remember ever hearing that phrase before, and I was curious as to whether or not God had really said it. Sure enough, when I typed the phrase into the Bible program on my phone, *Esther 4:14* popped up—the only verse in the Bible with that phrase.

When Mordecai sought out Esther on behalf of the Jews, it was a perilous time for the chosen people of God. As Mordecai told Esther, "Who knows whether you have come to the kingdom *for such a time as this?*" God had a purpose for Esther, and I realized how fitting that phrase would be for a group of successful businesswomen. Still, I said, "Lord, how can I give this message without studying and preparing for it?"

When I walked into the meeting room, one of the leaders came up to me and asked if I would mind waiting for a while before delivering my message. They had been honored by a surprise visit of a highly anointed missionary who had a healing ministry and who wanted to pray for the women and share some of her testimony. While she did that, I sat quietly in the back as God gave me the entire message: "For Such a Time as This." I now marvel at how that same message began to saturate the Body of Christ all over the world. From that time until now, I have heard numerous pastors, evangelists, and prophets speak that same declaration, and it has been very fitting, indeed! When the Holy Spirit speaks to us, we need to be willing to act on His agenda instead of our own. Hearing His voice is critical to fulfilling our destiny in Him!

Throughout my journey with our heavenly Father, I have heard His quiet, *whispering voice,* and I have been moved by His love and mercy. I realized that I have not always listened to His *whispers,* but I know that when I do, I am blessed beyond measure. There is nothing as comforting in this earthly life than spending time with the Lord. When we listen to Him, He will guide us on a path of spiritual fulfillment that will exceed all understanding. I encourage you to put the heavenly Father, His Son, and the Holy Spirit first in your life when it comes to your family, your finances, and your education, and He will guide you through the struggles of life, just like He has done for me.

Preparation for a Battle with the Enemy

The greatest calling in my life has been to follow Jesus Christ. I was ordained for the ministry under Pat Harrison, the daughter of Kenneth Hagin Sr. and the wife of Buddy Harrison, publisher/founder of Harrison House Publishing. It's interesting to note that almost all of those called to this ministry had an anointing to prophesy in rhyme, as did I. When we attended assemblies, it was common to both get and receive a word under that kind of anointing. I was licensed in 2002 and ordained in 2004, and I continued under Pastor Terry and Becky Roberts at Faith Christian Family Church (FCFC), in Warrenton, Missouri, who served one church in two separate locations, the Wentzville and Warrenton campuses, with close to two thousand members. During that time, I also ministered in many different denominations as Rainbow the Musical Clown, bringing the Gospel to a Catholic Church School, I taught and preached in the Methodist Church, in Presbyterian churches, and in churches in other states.

God had a purpose for me, and this is what I have done in preparation to answering my call. If I had to define a call from God in any given area, I would say that I am equipped to teach, instruct, counsel, and impart what was imparted to me in the Body of Christ for over fifty years. I have a prophetic gift, and I have operated in that anointing. The last time Pastor Harold came to my church, Oceans Unite Christian Center, in Vero Beach, Florida, he spoke over me that I had a calling in prayer. That is a calling I want to honor to the best of my ability.

I believe we all have the calling to prayer, and as we develop our relationship with the unction of the Holy Spirit, we will see much more of a demonstration of His power with signs and wonders released in our communities.

If I were to define my call, it would be this: to manifest Jesus and to destroy the works of the devil. In 2013, Doug and I came to Vero Beach, and I believe God strategically placed us here to grow and equip Oceans Unite, where we have served for three years. Now finishing the final leg of Bible College, I hope to be instrumental in teaching Bible school, e-courses, counseling, and so on, continuing to equip, grow, and ensure that we thrive according to the vision God has given to Pastor Alex and Oceans Unite Christian Center.

As a believer, it has always been important to me to have clarity in hearing God's voice and obeying His direction throughout my Christian walk. It was not unusual for me to hear His voice, but it's a privilege afforded to every one of God's children. It would have been beyond comprehension for me to be deaf to His instruction. Jesus was speaking to the Jews when He said, "And other sheep I have which are not of this fold; them also I must bring, and they will hear My voice; and there will be one flock and one shepherd" (John 10:16). He also told them, "But you do not believe, because you are not My sheep.... My sheep hear My voice, and I know them, and they follow Me" (John 10:26–27).

Preparation for Spiritual Leadership

Home Fellowships "U Group Church"

While Jesus was here, He and His disciples went from house to house and from home to home teaching, fellowshiping, and breaking bread together. How far have we strayed from the simplicity of His Gospel? To be united in Him is to be in unity with one another. I feel so blessed to meet on the Lord's Day with my fellow believers for corporate worship and for teaching from our pastor. God has set in the Body some as apostles, some as prophets, some as evangelists, some as pastors, and some as teachers, and God is a God of order.

I love gleaning from all of these anointings, but we also gather for corporate prayer several times a week to cover each other, our community, and our world. Along with these blessings comes the highlight of my week: Every Wednesday evening, we attend our home cell meetings. In this place, we meet from house to house and from home to home. People are placed in U Groups according to their neighborhoods, so we can get to know and serve each other on a different and more personal level. We are called a U Group Church, and the benefits are beyond description. In this setting, we grow together, we grow up, and we grow out. Our numbers stay small, like the twelve disciples, and as we grow, we multiply. We are training up and sending out in the way Jesus taught us when He said, "Go into all the world and make disciples of every nation" (see Matthew 28:19). It not only unites us, but it teaches us how to function as a body. The greatest benefit to me is the ;lve we have for one another. Jesus said, "By this all will know that you are My disciples, if you have love for one another" (John 13:35).

When we get together as a U Group, we start by worshiping, and "Make Me a House of Prayer" is our theme song. Prayer is not a chore but a celebration of our communion with God and with each other. We practice the verse that says, "And over all these virtues put on love, which binds them all together in perfect unity" (Colossians 3:14 NIV). We are told in the Old Testament, "Behold, how good and how pleasant it is for brethren to dwell together in unity" (Psalm 133:1). This, too, has helped me to prepare for my mission to serve at the House of Transfiguration. The willingness to give to others is a blessing from God. When we help others, we are following an action of love. I praise God for all of his blessings and His purpose for my life.

Love Defined

As I became older and a little wiser, I expected and accepted family to be a normal part of my life, but my appreciation came full circle when I realized how short life is. Being a phlebotomist and an EKG tech exposed me to death, and I observed many people entering into eternity while surrounded by friends and loved ones. Yes, they felt love and comfort, but moments before taking their last breath, it was obvious that their family members were the ones they wanted to see most before passing on. I observed many kinds of love, and I began to do a study about this mysterious, lingering, vital need everyone pursues in life. I discovered five Greek root words defining very different meanings of love. The first was taken from "mania": *manic love.* The word "lust" is probably not strong enough to describe it; "obsession" is closer to the meaning. This is the love of possession. It is generally seen as taking over the "lover," like insanity. *Mania* is translated as "madness" and "beside yourself" as referenced in Acts 26:24, where Paul was accused of being insane as he witnessed to Festus.

The second word, *eros*, is the root for the English word "erotic," but it does not describe sexual love only. It actually describes all emotional love; it is the feeling of love. *Eros* love is that insatiable desire to be near the target of one's love. It's the love that says, "I love how you make me feel." This type of love is not found in the Bible, but it may be the closest to defining how mankind experiences what is commonly called the "fruit and flowers" of a new relationship. *Eros* is neither good nor bad, but it can change quickly with unstable emotions. Many scholars believe *eros* thinking affects our interactions in sex and intimacy.

Philos love, or brotherly/friendship, describes the love between two people who have common interests and experiences, or a fondness for one another, and it will generally grow over time. In Revelation 3:19, Jesus said, "Those whom I love I rebuke and discipline. So be earnest, and repent" (NIV).

Storgae love is commonly called "motherly love," and it is based entirely on the relationship between the lover and the one who is loved It is one of the stronger types of loves, because it involves a commitment that relies on only one trait of the receiver—that he or she is dependent on the one who loves. This type of love can be toxic in a marriage because it lacks relationship between a man and wife. Instead, it looks more like mother/son or father/daughter role, which distorts the husband/wife relationship and can prove to be destructive.

Lastly, we come to *agape* love, which is entirely about the lover, having absolutely nothing to do with the one being loved. *Agape* love, in its purest form, requires no payment or favor in response, and it is the most common word used for God's love for us. John 3:16 tells us: "For God so loved the world that He gave His only begotten Son, that whoever believes in Him should not perish but have everlasting life." This is the same kind of love we are commanded to have for one another. Unconditional love, *agape* is frequently translated as "charity," and it is freely given and freely committed to.

Ultimately, this brings me to my own reckoning with my emotions and my relationship with God. Our need for love is normally sought for in ways that lead to momentary satisfaction, but this often results in disappointment and failure. Because of our penchant for fairy tales and movies with happy endings, hoping against hope, we take the plunge and find that love is blinder than we thought.

I had experienced two marriages, two beautiful children, a new home, and good provision, and yet my own love was not enough. After endless prayers, and a stubborn determination to stay in a loveless marriage, I was deserted, abandoned, and totally defeated. Yet, in the midst of this drama, God did what no man could do. He helped me in ways that surpassed my comprehension and blessed me beyond what I could ask or even think. He truly became my Husband, my Provider, and the Lover of my soul. After years of rejection and degradation, my relationship with Jesus began to heal the deep wounds and ugly scars in my heart. The years of Bible study, fellowship, home U Groups, attending church, and reading the Word of God finally took root. God's plans and purposes finally began to surface through intimate instruction and a closer walk with the Holy Spirit. Finally, what had been there all along manifested, and the veil over my eyes fell with happy tears as I stepped into another dimension.

Because of the healing I received from my own experiences and heartbreaks, I can now encourage you to seek comfort and restoration in the Lord. Lean on Him, get to know Him, and hold steadfast to the promises He has given you. It is important to keep in mind that we do not truly have control of any of our relationships with other people, whether it be with our husband, wife, children, friends, coworkers, or individuals in our church family. We must work on our relationships with others and stay steadfast in prayer for the people who are part of our lives. Seeking full control is a form of rebellion: "For rebellion is as the sin of witchcraft, and stubbornness is as iniquity and idolatry" (1 Samuel 15:23). Other people may disappoint you and reject you, but God never intended for you to raise them. He is a perfect Father, and He perfectly knows how to raise His own children. We are simply called to love others and trust Him to do what we cannot. He will never leave us nor forsake us. What He begins, He will perfect until He returns, and His Word never returns void.

Love is your greatest gift and your greatest commission. Do not worry about changing others; just let go and let God do what only He can. Grab hold of Him and never let go. I learned this fact many years ago when I realized that I do not have unlimited control over the actions or emotions of others. During challenging, emotional times, we must draw closer to God and realize that out of the worst situations in life, there are rewards that we must learn to recognize and appreciate, for they, too, are gifts from God. Remember that serving others as Jesus did will catapult us to a higher calling in life.

In Isaiah 61:3, the prophet declared, "The Spirit of the Lord God...gives them beauty for ashes, the oil of joy for mourning, the garment of praise for the spirit of heaviness; they will be called oaks of righteousness, a planting of the Lord for the display of His splendor." Jesus is glorified in you, as you become an ambassador of His love. This is the greatest commandment, and as it is fulfilled, you will be eternally fulfilled, as well.

Prayer

Dear holy Abba Father, You are a wonder to behold. In all of Your creation, Your endless story iss told. Your majesty, Your tapestry, and Your creative flair floods my heart with gratitude and fills my mouth with prayer. How can it be... Your majesty, as Lord of lords and King of kings, that I have been adopted into this place of royal dreams? That I can call you Abba Father with praise and thanksgiving? My very own Daddy, my Abba, Your idea, Your song. I can't wrap my mind around how You called me to belong. I was so unworthy, and I am unworthy still...but You placed Your seal upon me by Your covenant and will. All the sin that weighed me down, You cleansed me from by Your grace. So I come into the throne room and take my rightful place: the place You choose for Your family, sanctified with holy blood. O Lamb of God, Anointed One, by Your redeeming blood, sealed by Your Holy Spirit, dear Abba Father, You have truly set me free, and I am overwhelmed as to where You have seated me. I praise You, Lord, as You rule and reign forever throughout eternity.

Notes

Notes

Chapter 10

The Real Mission

In this you greatly rejoice, though now for a little while, if need be, you have been grieved by various trials, that the genuineness of your faith, being much more precious than gold that perishes, through it is tested by fire, may be found to praise, honor, and glory at the revelation of Jesus Christ.

—1 Peter 1:6–7 NKJV

Change is an inevitable part of life. In fact, from the time we are born, we go through a metamorphism that shapes us and transforms us throughout our earthly existence. At times, the change can be so subtle that we do not notice it is happening to us at all. Then there are other times when change can make us feel so vulnerable, helpless, lost, and desperate for direction. Our hearts can be broken by change, and when this happens, we must rely on the Lord Jesus Christ to take us to a place of peace and comfort. If we look at the change and disappointments in our lives with a positive perspective, they can provide opportunities for us to serve God in all His glory.

This is exactly what happened to Doug and me as we faced losing our home and business, which we believed was a ministry of God. The loss of our home and business was beyond our control; it was subject to the economic conditions of the times. Doug and I were never extravagant, and almost everything we purchased was secondhand from a resale shop or garage sale, but to us, our blessings overflowed. God blessed us, and fifteen wooded acres were miraculously placed in our care. We both loved the woods, and we were nestled between two ridges with creek beds on either side. The trees were outstanding. Tall oaks and their plentiful acorns drew in wildlife in abundance. Deer, turkey, pheasants, squirrels, rabbits, bobcats, fox, and even a variety of snakes graced our little paradise. The tall black walnut, the sugar maple, Eastern redbuds, birch, persimmon trees, and flowering dogwoods would beckon nearly 435 species of native Missouri birds to our delight. The songbirds and the beautiful cardinals would bring a delightful backdrop when the winter snowfalls filled the air and blanketed the woods with breathtaking beauty. God is an Artist like no other, and nothing could compare to His majestic flair.

In the spring, our flowering mimosa and blossoming magnolia trees would call in a variety of hummingbirds that would never disappoint as the woods came alive with a magic of its own. There aren't words to describe the beauty and serenity we enjoyed. We worked from sunrise to past sunset, but the symphony of God's extravagant creation filled our hearts with an abundance of peace and joy. We were definitely in our element, enjoying the fruits of our labors and God's bountiful gifts of our Missouri home. The Bible says we were created for His pleasure, but this world was created for ours. We so enjoyed what He lavished upon us, including our regal Goldendoodles and Labradoodles. Yes, Faun Haven had been appropriately named by Doug, and AMEN Dogs meant, "Let it be so." We worked hard to build our dream, and we were blessed beyond measure.

An Unexpected Truth

For almost two decades, we toiled with a vengeance until we were suddenly blindsided with a rude awakening. We began to realize we were no longer spring chickens, and our youth was beginning to falter. Our last two years presented many obstacles and challenges, and it seemed as if we were blindsided by circumstances beyond our control. For two years in a row, Doug slipped on the ice while cleaning the kennels, and each time he broke several ribs. Then he had several major surgeries and underwent unbearable pain along with a laboring recovery. Around the same time, I got up one morning and couldn't walk. After seeing several specialists and taking countless tests, they determined my thyroid was barely functioning, but it was overworking itself. They told me if I had waited much longer to seek medical attention, I could have died.

If Louie, whom I introduced earlier in the book, had not been with us to run the kennels, I don't know what we would have done. On top of it all, after a brutal bypass vascular surgery, Doug developed MERSA MASA and a factor five blood clotting disorder. The doctors said he was dying and there was nothing more they could do. We still had our foster teens, and we had to find placements for them. That alone was heartrending but only the beginning of the changes coming to Faun Haven. God had always been with us, but now it seemed He was nowhere to be found. We cried, prayed, and begged Him to rescue us, but we found ourselves in a downward spiral. Many miracles happened during this time, but none were in the way we expected. Our foster teens were reunited with their families, Doug was supernaturally healed, and God brought many people our way who would help us with dismantling the kennels, placing the dogs, and closing our businesses. The stark reality was that we had gone from middle-aged newlyweds to senior citizens in the twinkling of an eye. Not only were we getting old, but we found ourselves in the middle of a recession that lasted ten years.

Due to a lack of banking regulations in 2008, interest rates skyrocketed. Compounded with hedge funds and inflation, the financial crisis spurred a loss of over ten million homes and more than 170,000 small businesses folded. The crisis lasted ten years, but to Doug and me, it felt like it happened overnight. Not understanding that God was working on our behalf and the plans to uproot us were beyond what we could have imagined, the dream and ministry we built was dismantled. It seemed that in a heartbeat, we lost it all: our home, our businesses, our dogs, the foster teens, and even most of our furnishings. Missouri had been our homeland for generations, and pulling up roots was beyond description. It was an emotional upheaval for our foster teens and for us. They, and many before them, had called Faun Haven home. It was a place to return for special occasions and holidays, or just for simple prayer and hugs. Change was not easy for any of us, but like lumps of clay, God had been molding us with His hands, inspiring us with His love, and creating a work of art whose sole purpose was to serve and glorify the Lord.

The Potter and the Dizzy Clay

Said the Potter to the clay,
"I'm going to work on you today."
Said the clay with much disdain,
"Here goes another day of pain."

Said the Potter with a smile,
"I'll only work on you a while."
Said the clay with a frown,
"You'll turn my whole world upside down."

Said the Potter with a nod,
"Trust me, clay, you know I'm God."
Said the clay, "I know You're GOD,
"BUT must You POKE and push and prod?"

The Potter gently took the clay
And worked a little every day.
Although the clay was stiff at first,
He finally yields, but it gets worse.

The Potter starts to spin the wheel,
And the dizzy clay begins to reel.
The skillful Potter cups His hands
And watches as the clay expands.

With gentle pressure and timely spins,
A GENIUS plan of change begins,
And then the clay began to pout:
"I think You've turned me inside out."

"This isn't what I thought I'd be.
"I think I know what's best for me."
The Potter put him on the shelf
And let the clay assess himself.

With time, the clay was very still
And told the Potter, "Do Your will."
The Potter took His paint and brush
To give that clay His finished touch.

The clay had gone from empty mire
To moving through the Potter's fire,
But when everything was said and done,
That clay was shining in the sun.

Holding soil and growing flowers,
Equipped to withstand storms and showers,
Filled with beauty, the Clay now knows
The Potter's hand brings joys untold.

And GLORY to the Potter's skill,
As the clay surrenders to HIS WILL.
The Potter's gift is beyond measure
Where earthen vessels hold priceless treasure.

From the Potter with the clay
Come the children of the day,
Yielded vessels, holy hands,
Trusting in the Potter's plan.

Inspired by the Master of All Creation,
Faun Collett

So it was with us, and soon we found that the Potter had other work for us to complete. It was painful to leave our church family in Warrenton, Missouri. We had been blessed with an abundance of love and care. Just like molded clay, we had been shaped and formed in this spiritual place. We had planted, sowed, toiled, and bonded with ties that would never be broken, and we all felt the void of the coming distance. Sometimes it seemed unbearable. However, time did not afford us the luxury of procrastination, and we found ourselves at the crossroads of change. Before we knew it, we looked like the Beverly Hillbillies of days gone by, as we loaded up a small U-Haul with our few meagre belongings, and with the help of our two best friends, we headed off to Florida. My daughter rescued us with a rental she and her husband owned, and we settled into our new beginning. God knew the plans for us, and they were exciting, abundantly above and beyond what we could have even asked or thought.

We have been in the Sunshine State now going on eight years. I have watched my grandchildren grow, and we've had wonder-filled times with them and my wonderful caring daughter. My sister Carla and her family followed suit and arrived in Florida one year after we got here; they bought a house just one mile from ours. We go to the same church, Oceans Unite Christian Center, and we are both very active in ministry. Although we knew God had worked many miracles for us, it was also evident we were in a battle and challenged by the enemy of our soul.

Doug and I faced obstacles that could only be overcome by the blood of the Lamb and the word of our testimony. Family relationships were shaken, and heartrending darts were hurled at us with a vengeance. Even though we recognized they were spiritual attacks, it was almost unbearable. Divisions, accusations, misunderstandings, and disagreements took a toll on us, as well as on our children and grandchildren. Feelings of rejection pulled at our hearts and theirs. It seemed that no matter how hard we tried, we were accused of abandoning some of them when we left our home in Missouri, and we were denied the joy of watching them grow and sharing their lives from then until now. That was a pain like no other, but it was just the beginning of many sorrows.

In 2017, Doug was diagnosed with tongue cancer, and it didn't look good. The ear, nose, and throat doctor refused to perform the surgery because the cancer was too close to Doug's throat, and so we were referred to a surgeon at the Mayo Clinic in Tampa, Florida. Although it would be risky, this doctor agreed to operate but it was a very trying ordeal. Not only was the clinic several hours away, the pre-op visits and road trips back and forth were very difficult for us. So many prayers went out, and the support from our church family and my family there in Florida brought God's undeniable intervention, and the surgery was an amazing success. In fact, it was a miracle from God, because Doug didn't even need chemo or radiation.

Two years later, I was taken to the hospital due to extreme pain in my back, and they found a large mass in my lung. At that point, we were faced with finding a doctor who would be accepted by Medicare, and the nightmare started all over again. After waiting many weeks to get in to see a pulmonary specialist, I was told I had inoperable Stage 4 lung cancer, that had spread to my lymph nodes. The doctor said there was nothing more he could do than refer me to an oncologist; if I chose to do nothing, I might have a year left to live. It was four months before I got approval and the results of the PET scan and found a doctor who could work with me. Five months later, I was back in the hospital coughing up blood and having difficulty breathing. The on-call doctor did a lifesaving procedure on me by freezing and cutting back a new fast-growing tumor that was blocking my airways. He cauterized the bleeding, but he said it was only a Band-Aid to hold me over until my pulmonary doctor returned from his vacation. From that time until now, I have been in a life-and-death struggle. *Every time natural circumstances try to overtake me, I go to the Great Physician, Jesus Christ. He makes free house calls, and He never disappoints.*

I have learned to fight the fight of faith with new resolve, speak to the mountains with authority straight from the Author and Finisher of my faith, and speak a contradiction to the plans of the evil one. I don't know how long I have left on this earth, but I am confident of this: If God is for me, nothing can or will stand against me. Whose report will I believe—the doctors' report or the Word of God? Hands-down, I will believe the Word, and I know the Truth that sets me free. I have nothing against doctors and medicine, and I am thankful for the healing they offer, but I know where my true healing comes from!

Prophetic Word Given to Me

Both have been set before you, and I would not call you to build without a plan. When man begins to build, Babel towers and the author of confusion sets his seal, but the sands of time pull down the lofty schemes of man. Who shall exalt his plans above My head? My cornerstone has been laid, My support beams are in place, and My architecture is sound. The sound of My voice from the core is crying out; I have prepared a place for you, and where I am, you must be also. Build on the same side of the structure so that you do not lose sight of each other, and allow My Spirit to guide you. Nothing done by My hand is in vain—substance and structure, mortar and brick, build, bring, restore, heal the sick. Leave sin outside, turn on the Light. Remember Me—fight the fight.

> Except the LORD builds the house, they labor in vain who build it.
>
> —Psalm 127:1 AMPC

God Saves the Best for Last

Before Doug and I dreamed we would ever leave Missouri, I had a dream/vision of a round house with a conference room in the middle of the house. In the center of the conference room, a tall tree grew through the top of the atrium, and it was strong, healthy, and beautiful. I thought it was a picture of what God wanted us to build for aged-out foster youth in Missouri, never dreaming it was a picture of what God had planned for us in Florida. After relocating to the Sunshine State, I settled into Oceans Unite Christian Center; the moment I walked in the place, I knew I was home. From the beginning, I knew this special house of worship was a God-centered church, and the pastor was there to teach, preach, and serve the Lord. The pastor is one who believes in empowering the congregation with biblical knowledge from the Word of God. He encourages biblical training and educational opportunities for anyone who wishes to seek a better understanding of God, the Son, and the Holy Spirit. I took every e-course, participated in every event, and even signed up for discipleship training college (DTC), graduating three years later. I was given a leadership pin, although no one was certain of what I was leading, but I was sure that I was still being molded and used for the glory of God.

Pastor Alex probably said it best when he prophesied over me during one of our services. He said I was like a hidden servant, under the covers, under the radar, but always helping people and seeking to do God's will, and that God was still going to use me, even in my old age. Hence, I would soon find out that my work for the Lord was not finished. I am so blessed to be in a church where the Holy Spirit is welcomed and worshiped, a church that is focused on making a difference in the community for the glory of God and the harvesting of souls to fill God's Kingdom. Such commitment takes faith and requires an outreach mission to a community that provides assistance to the weakest among us.

With much prayer and planning on Pastor Alex's part, the need to provide a physical, safe space where spiritual guidance and direction could be taught to those in need was eventually birthed and called the House of Transfiguration. Miracles have taken place in this mission, and lives have been changed, and I am sure that God's purpose for the mission has just begun. Doug and I were asked to move into the octagon building to oversee the land and to work with the women who would enter the House of Transfiguration. I had the privilege of writing some of the curriculum for this ministry, especially the Morning Watch, which began each day with prayer. I was one of the counselors for the ladies, there daily to encourage and mentor each of them. Doug was busy planting flowers, feeding the chickens, and repairing a few things when needed. What a blessing it is to work for the Lord, and to know that you have been instrumental in helping others come to Christ.

When Doug and I moved onto the grounds of the mission, it was at the beginning of the beginning. The land was newly acquired, and change was in the air. So many dedicated and faithful volunteers rallied around us and began the remodel efforts of the Octagon House and the long ranch house behind us called the House of Transfiguration. The zeal of God consumed us, and the fire of God was burning in each one of us. The abbreviation for the House of Transfiguration is HOT, and HOT it is! Pastor Alex, Tara, Doug, and I sat down for a few planning meetings, and God set things into motion. The process of renovating the House of Transfiguration took on an urgency like a whirlwind. Since its conception, HOT has been expanded with two add-on bedrooms for mothers and children so that more little ones can now be accommodated.

A transformational program and curriculum was created to meet the needs of the women who entered the program and living quarters at the House of Transfiguration. The residents are required to participate in a faith-based transformational, educational environment that changes the lives of those who come to us. These priceless souls come to the program broken, with no structure in their lives. For most of them, their lives were spinning out of control, and without intervention, hopelessness was inevitable. Fortunately, this special place brings change to those who enter the program, as well as those who provide counseling and teaching at the House of Transfiguration. Recently, three ladies graduated from the yearlong program. They were taught life-management and parenting skills, and they were given jobs in the community so they, too, could fulfill the purpose that God had for each of them. Most importantly, they have accepted the Lord, and their lives have been changed because of God's forgiving love.

A Closer Walk with Him

Far too soon, my excitement at the possibilities of serving the Lord at the House of Transfiguration took on a whole new dimension. Because of my cancer diagnosis, my body has become weaker, but my spirit and desire to serve Him grows stronger every day. I speak of Him to strangers, to family members, and to anyone who will listen to my testimony of His love, mercy, and grace. My role at the House of Transfiguration has changed. Now I tell the mission residents how wonderful they are, how important they are to the Lord, and how grateful I am that I had been given the opportunity to know them.

I don't know how long I have left on this earth, but I am confident of this: I know where my true healing comes from, and it is through my covenant with Jesus, my Healer. He paid for all of it, and I'm eager to receive all He has done for me. By His stripes, I'm healed. It's true that I'm in a fight of faith, and it's not a dance. Because of my treatment plans, doctor visits, scans, etc., my pastor asked me to take some time off with HOT and concentrate on my healing and writing my books. As of now, I am the published author of *The Potter and the Dizzy Clay,* and I have *The Jesus Whisperer* ready now for publication.

God has given me everything I need pertaining to life and godliness, and His grace to me has been amazing. I am so thankful that He is my God and Savior. My last thoughts are simple at best, but perhaps the most profound thing I can share with you, my dear reader, is that death is inevitable! I want to encourage you to think about the promises of God. He sent His Son, Jesus Christ, to die a physical death so we could have everlasting life. In John 14:2–3, Jesus said,

"In My Father's house are many mansions; if it were not so, I would have told you. I go to prepare a place for you. And if I go and prepare a place for you, I will come again and receive you to Myself; that where I am, there you may be also." This is God's promise of everlasting life, and I am excited as I listen for His *quiet whisper* that reassures me that I will live with Him forevermore.

PROPHECY

August 16, 2017 , Pastor Harold Weisz

Pastor Harold began to sing, "Cast your burdens onto Jesus, for He cares for you" as he laid his hands on me. He said, " Because what you're doing is you're clinging to it. You're holding onto things, you're holding onto the past. You're wanting the things of the past that went wrong to come right. God says, 'I move you on!' God says 'they will follow you. You won't turn back. They will follow you, you won't turn back.' Listen to me. Do you understand what I'm saying? You're going to set a new standard for family and friends, OK? Because the Lord's got a ministry for you and it's a ministry of prayer, and I see you moving towards the sick and hospitals, and I see you very compassionate and God's got this for you, but there's things in the past that He wants you to let go of, because the past is always like a ball and chain...not in the Kingdom of God, but of other things. Now my hands have remained upon that spot all this time. There is power all the time; I can feel it all the time. Did you come in here with discomfort or pain or anything? (I answered, but couldn't make out the answer) and Pastor Harold said, " I can hear that American accent," and laughed, saying "Somehow that reminded me I am in America. Sound said "USA" and it sounds so good. My goodness, the lady opens her mouth and I can just hear it! OK, now "Let go of the past and take hold of the future and press on towards the goal," says the Lord, and people will follow you. You won't have to follow. You are cared for all the days of your life, therefore this YOKE is BROKEN in Jesus' Name!

Thank You, Lord Jesus!!

A final message to my readers is simple but powerful. Don't live in the past or dwell on what cannot be changed or rectified. Stay steadfast in prayer, listen to God's quiet whispers, and focus on eternal life not the unchangeable past.

About the Author

Faun Collett is an accomplished author and speaker who has raised the dead, has released healing to the sick, and believes it's time for the demonstration of the power God desires His people to have if they will listen and discern His voice. As an accomplished author and speaker, Faun has won the distinguished Editor's Choice Award from the National Library of Poetry, Faun was published in five anthologies in the National Library of Congress. and she is the author of *The Jesus Whisperer* and *The Potter and the Dizzy Clay.*

Faun and her husband, Douglas, have been actively serving others as foster parents, foster parent trainers, and facilitators of a step-down/recovery program. They created a pilot program for the Warren County alternative schools and worked with at-risk students, abused youth from youth services, and A+ honor students to mentor struggling youth. They have boarded, raised, and trained service and support dogs through their Faun Haven board and bread and their 501 C3 Academy Missouri Educational Network of Graduate Dogs Inc. They have also provided shelter and provision for many homeless, abused, and abandoned youth.

Faun and Douglas currently reside on the premises of the Real Mission. They serve in any capacity needed to build up, encourage, and equip those whom the Lord brings their way. Their model is to grow up, to grow together, and to grow out, and their portion is the love of Christ. The Real Mission is a ministry of Ocean's Unite Christian Center Church in Indian River County. This retreat for women and children focuses on life skills and helping the residents to discover their own God-ordained unique capabilities to equip them for a hope, future, and destiny of their own. Love, peace, and support undergirds them and gives them family ties that no one but God can produce.

Faun lives in Vero Beach, Florida, with her husband and their adorable multi-poo, Molly. Faun is a licensed and ordained minister with an adventurous spirit and a ready smile. She lives her life as a disciple of Christ with an evangelistic passion and has a calling on her life to serve others. She receives prophetic rhyme from the Holy Spirit and hears from Him daily. The word *poem* comes from a root word that likens itself to one of the earliest descriptions of God as Maker, Creator. The Bible tells us we are God's poem and that His creative gifts have been placed and expressed in His creation. Often the prophetic gift Faun has received is expressed in rhyme, and the prophecy is straight from the heart of the Father.

You may contact Faun at:
thejesuswhisperer@gmail.com
www.thejesuswhisperer.org